SOUP
Glorious Soup

SOUP
Glorious Soup

Annie Bell

Photography by Richard Jung

Kyle Books

For Rothko

Published in 2011 by Kyle Books
www.kylebooks.com

Distributed by National Book Network, 4501 Forbes Boulevard, Suite 200, Lanham, MD 20706, (800) 462-6420

First published in Great Britain in 2010 by Kyle Cathie Limited, 23 Howland Street, London W1T 4AY

ISBN 978-1-906868-29-1

Editor: Vicky Orchard   *Design:* Jane Humphrey   *Photography:* Richard Jung   *Styling:* Gabi Tubbs   *Food styling:* Annie Rigg
Copy editor: Catherine Ward   *Production:* Gemma John

Library of Congress Control Number: 2011926473

Color reproduction by Sang Choy in Singapore
Printed in China by C&C Offset Printing Co., Ltd.

ACKNOWLEDGMENTS Many thanks to those small independent shops who keep the flag flying, and who kindly allowed us to photograph within: Patricia Michelson and La Fromagerie, Marylebone; Fiona O'Callaghan and James Knight of Mayfair; David House, Glen Kirton and Allens butcher, and Charlie Boxer and Italo Deli.
With many thanks to Kyle Cathie and Judith Hannam, Commissioning Editor, to Vicky Orchard, Editor, to Julia Barder, Sales and Marketing Director, and to Victoria Scales for publicity. With particular thanks also to Jane Humphrey for designing the book, to Gabi Tubbs for her art direction, to Richard Jung for the photography, to Annie Rigg for cooking and presenting the dishes, and to Rachel Wood, also to Angela Mason. And as ever, to Jonnie, Louis and Rothko, for settling to bowl after bowl over many years.

Contents

A recent American university study came to the conclusion that we can all be defined as particular character types depending on our soup preference. Aside from marvelling that any educational establishment can find the resources to carry out this kind of research, it left me feeling I must be suffering from a personality disorder. I, for one, cannot choose. If I was asked to select between a smooth silky onion soup, a gazpacho, a hearty lentil soup, a thin hot and sour Thai broth, a luxurious garlic-rich *bourride*, a chicken noodle soup and a smoked haddock chowder, I would be left tongue-tied and trembling. Thankfully I don't have to choose.

Soup encompasses every possible conception of liquid, and increasingly not-so-liquid sustenance, catering to every whimsical mood and occasion. But most importantly, it is so often a way of making the best of whatever ingredients we have on hand.

This is not to say it is a vehicle for using up odds and ends, although on occasion you can achieve very fine results by marrying whatever you have in the fridge. Countless soups in this book have been born out of an enjoyable early evening hour spent hovering over the stove, adding, tasting, simmering, adding and tasting. But never should this involve "bits of this and bits of that" which are past their prime; fill a pot with second-rate ingredients and you will get a second-rate soup. The one exception to the rule is a vegetable that has a good flavor but a poor texture, that will make an excellent creamed soup once it has been puréed and sieved. But if the flavor isn't there in the first place, you won't turn water into wine.

The savvy home cook will surely embrace a type of "soup cycle," the way it, and its ingredients, fit into our weekly repertoire of meals. Any household who regularly roasts a chicken, should certainly make a logical leap and decide to simmer a pot of stock at the end using the bird's carcass. Slightly stale bread can also be turned into a virtue, something not lost on French patisseries where the faintly burned or day-old loaves are sold in a basket labelled as "*pain au soupe,*" for crumbling into a *pot au feu* or a *poule au pot* to stretch it out. But aside from such frugality, a beautiful soup begins with beautiful ingredients.

This doesn't necessarily mean expensive. Soups based on lentils and beans, and vegetables such as carrots, celery and onions, have humble roots. But others such as fish soups, and ones containing lots of cheese or a large amount of herbs will be among the most luxurious dishes you can imagine. Either way, the starting point is to go shopping.

I am showing my age when I reminisce that shopping for food as a child meant a stroll down a main street of shops, a trip in turn to the greengrocer, the butcher, the fishmonger, the baker and the grocer with its shelves stacked with artfully packaged dried beans, lentils and rice, spices and flour. Even though such shopping today is the stuff of weekend jaunts and holidays when there is the time to indulge, I still map out what I am going to buy in this way.

Aside from the quality of the produce, the experience itself is so pleasurable. Being able to look at ingredients, to admire the way they are displayed and packaged, seeking advice from those selling them for inspiration on how to cook them, just engaging each other with the ingredient at the center of the conversation, is a precursor to cooking it.

Hence the chapters that follow evoke a stroll down a traditional village street, each shop doing what it does best. Most soups will contain a selection of ingredients, but for every one there is normally a single ingredient at its heart that relates to one particular shop – be it leeks from the greengrocer for a *potage parmentier*, some mussels from the fishmonger for a *moules marinière* or a hunk of mature farmhouse Cheddar for a cauliflower cheese soup. I believe if you approach soups in this way, centering them on one fine ingredient and letting that lead, rather than as a way of using up unwanted odds and ends, then you will create something special.

There is always an element of fashion within cooking, and soups mirror this more than many other foods. Aside from approaching them from a different angle than our forebears for whom soups were most often a means of frugality, there has been a broadening of our perception of soup in recent years.

Traditionally soups were either thin, creamed or consommés, whereas today they embrace all kinds of dishes that are halfway to being stews. I adore these kind of soups, a mass of vegetables and bites of meat, often with lots of extra virgin olive oil and chopped herbs.

The dividing line between "is it or isn't it a soup?", for me is whether or not you would ladle it over buttery potatoes or rice. If, despite its heartiness, you would eat it with a spoon and some bread on the side, then in my eyes it qualifies as a soup. So many of the recipes in this book, and in particular in the butcher and fishmonger chapters, are main course material. There are also classic creamed or puréed soups, and others that broaden traditional perceptions – a jellied red pepper and tequila soup for instance, which can be eaten scooped onto fine slices of toast, or a French onion soup baked in the oven, that is something like a savory bread pudding.

I am more inclined to serve soup as the star dish with some cheese to follow than to make it the first course of a larger meal. It fits so well into family life – my love of soups was strengthened further with the arrival of my children who are habitual "dippers." They love nothing more than dunking a piece of bread into soup, a great way of deceiving them into eating all sorts of nutritious vegetables they might otherwise turn their noses up at. It's an excuse for a trip to the baker to pick up a well-crafted, rustic loaf that succeeds in being moist and chewy at the same time, with a crust that invites your teeth to grip and tear it apart. In a perfect world it will have been baked in a wood-fired oven, its base covered with a pale brownish-gray dusting of ashes, all of which adds to the flavor. Treat yourself to a particularly fine loaf or two, with rosemary, olives or garlic, sunflower seeds and spelt, or walnuts, or a loaf that includes potato or corn, or a sourdough boule, all of which add to the general *joie de vivre* of a large, warming bowlful.

I also love dressing soups up, whether it's a fried garlic crouton resting in the bottom of the bowl to soak it up, or a dollop of crème fraîche mashed with Roquefort cheese that melts into it. There are lots of suggestions for little asides and frills in the recipes that follow, but few are essential and if all you are after is a really simple bowlful, then these can be left out. Otherwise, hidden treasures and surprises add to the interest, and that most comforting of meals, a soup supper.

The Greengrocer

Of all the shops along the street, it is the greengrocer I find most alluring, with its damp, musty scent of earth clinging to roots and crates piled precariously high. A good greengrocer is an extension of a market garden, at any time of year a window onto the season, a reminder of what is at its best and what we should be enjoying at that particular time. There is hardly a vegetable that won't shine in a soup given the chance — a medium that takes what is fine and runs with it. We may not readily embrace the do-good austerity of raw vegetables, but soups play to their soft side — and encapsulate everything that we love about them in liquid, comfort form.

Tomato consommé

Serves 4

3½ pounds ripe plum tomatoes, halved
½ teaspoon sea salt

½ teaspoon sugar
4 small basil leaves (optional), to serve

Place the tomatoes in a large saucepan, cover with a lid and heat very gently for 30–40 minutes until soft, stirring occasionally. Line a sieve with a tea towel or with cheese cloth, set it over a bowl containing the salt and sugar and pour in the tomatoes and juice. Leave for a good hour, ideally overnight, so that as much of the juice as possible runs through the sieve.

Once you are ready to serve, stir the soup, taste for seasoning and reheat gently, or serve cold. Spoon into small cups and float a basil leaf on the surface of each cup if you wish. This is perfect served with the bruschettas (see below) and a radish salad on the side (see page 13).

On the side

Bruschetta with lima bean purée and tuscan kale

These are as hearty as the consommé is delicate, so they make a good contrast. As well as tuscan kale, red chard is another contender, but step up the quantity by about half and cook it for a few minutes less.

½ pound tuscan kale, stalks removed, washed
6 tablespoons extra virgin olive oil, plus
*   extra to serve*
sea salt

½ lemon
1 x 14-ounce can lima beans, drained and rinsed
1 garlic clove, peeled and coarsely chopped
8 slices of baguette, ½-inch thick

Bring a large pot of salted water to a boil, add the kale and boil for 10 minutes. Drain into a sieve and press out any excess liquid using a large spoon. Transfer to a chopping board and chop, and then place in a bowl. Dress with 2 tablespoons olive oil, a little salt and a squeeze of lemon juice. Leave to cool.

Place the lima beans in a food processor with the garlic, 4 tablespoons olive oil and some salt and process into a purée. Add the remaining lemon juice to taste.

To serve the bruschettas, toast the slices of baguette – you may find it easier to do this under the broiler than in a toaster. Lay the slices of toast out on a large plate, drizzle with a little olive oil, and then place a heaping teaspoon of the lima bean purée on top. Top this with a heaping teaspoon of the greens and drizzle with a little more oil.

This renders a tiny cup of crystal clear consommé — beauty before quantity. It is no more than the juice from fresh tomatoes, seasoned to bring out their flavor, so the only thing that really matters is the quality of that one ingredient. The rest of the tomato needn't go to waste however, you can press the pulp through a sieve and use it in a sauce.

Summer's day zucchini soup

Picture yourself in a hot, dusty city in southern Italy in the middle of summer. You chance across a backstreet restaurant with a couple of tables in the shade, with a limited menu, but featuring a most alluring bowl of chunky vegetable soup made early that morning. The soup has reached an ambient temperature now that it is lunchtime, scarcely cool. There is something about vegetable soups such as minestrone eaten at this temperature that combine the freshness of being newly cooked, with an added flavor and sweetness that intensifies upon cooling. Frying the zucchini until they are golden brings out their delicacy and succulence, and laced with basil purée this makes for a rich spoonful.

Serves 6

⅓ cup extra virgin olive oil, plus extra
for frying the zucchini
3½ pounds zucchini, ends removed, quartered
lengthways and sliced
sea salt, black pepper

5 garlic cloves, peeled and finely chopped
1 quart vegetable stock
½ cup basil leaves
a couple of squeezes of fresh lemon juice

You will need to cook the zucchini in batches. Heat a couple of tablespoons of olive oil in a large saucepan over medium heat, add about a third of the zucchini, season with salt and pepper and cook for 10–15 minutes until meltingly tender and golden. Cook the rest in the same manner, stirring in the garlic a couple of minutes before the end. You will find the batches brown more quickly as you proceed.

Return all the zucchini to the pan, add the stock and season generously with salt. Bring to a boil and then remove from the heat. Process half of the soup in a food processor, and then stir it back into the pan with the rest of the soup. Pour into a bowl and leave to cool.

Meanwhile, process the basil with ⅓ cup olive oil in a food processor until it becomes a textured purée. Stir half the basil purée into the soup and season to taste with lemon juice. Ladle the soup into bowls and serve the rest of the purée spooned over the top.

The Greengrocer

Chilled avocado soup

I have never been comfortable with the word "smoothie," but I guess this soup is closely affiliated – a blended, chilled soup, silky and pale green. The cucumber takes the place of stock here, lending itself to the soup's cool nature. To its credit, unlike many avocado soups that slowly turn a sludgy brown after an hour or so, this will be good for a day.

Serves 4

2 avocados, halved

3 cucumbers, ends discarded, peeled and
   cut into pieces

2 shallots, peeled and roughly chopped

1 tablespoon cider vinegar

3 tablespoons extra virgin olive oil, plus
   extra to serve

sea salt, black pepper

a dash of Tabasco

a few slivers of scallion

Scoop the avocado flesh into a blender, add all the remaining ingredients except the scallion and process until smooth. Transfer to a bowl, then cover and chill for a couple of hours. The soup should be eaten on the day it's made. Serve with a drizzle of olive oil and a few slivers of scallion. Accompany with smoked salmon and a little radish salad on the side (see below) if you wish.

On the side

Smoked salmon

black pepper

5 ounces sliced, smoked salmon, cut into wide strips

lemon wedges, to serve

Grind some black pepper over the smoked salmon and serve with the lemon wedges.

Radish salad

1 cup French breakfast radishes, trimmed and thinly sliced

2 tablespoons mayonnaise

sea salt

6 tablespoons alfalfa sprouts

Mix the radishes with the mayonnaise in a bowl and season to taste with salt. Place a tablespoon of alfalfa sprouts on four plates, spreading them out a little. Spoon the radish salad on top and scatter with a few more sprouts.

Jellied red pepper and tequila soup

A soup that stands close to the divide into the realms of mousses and patés. This is just as good spooned onto rice crackers, or scooped up with thin toast as it is eaten with a spoon. And it's light to boot.

Serves 6

4–5 tablespoons extra virgin olive oil

2 medium onions, peeled and chopped

3 garlic cloves, peeled and finely chopped

2 pounds sweet red peppers, core and seeds removed, coarsely chopped

½ pound ripe tomatoes, quartered

1 bay leaf

sea salt

5 sheets of gelatine (i.e. Dr. Oetker), cut into broad strips

2 tablespoons tequila

a squeeze of lime juice

To serve

crème fraîche or Greek yogurt

a few brightly colored petals (e.g. marigold, nasturtium, clover, rose, etc.)

Heat a couple of tablespoons of oil in a large pan over medium heat, add the onions and cook for about 5 minutes until softened and starting to brown, stirring occasionally. Stir in the garlic and cook for a minute or so, and then transfer everything to a large saucepan and set aside.

You will need to cook the peppers in batches. Add another couple of tablespoons of oil to the pan, and cook a half or one-third of the peppers for 6–8 minutes until lightly colored in patches, stirring occasionally. Transfer these to the saucepan with the onions, leaving the oil behind. Cook the rest of the peppers in the same way, adding more oil as necessary, and then place them in the saucepan.

Add the tomatoes, bay leaf, ¾ cup of water and some salt to the saucepan. Bring to a boil, and then cover and cook over low heat for 20 minutes. Towards the end of this time, place the gelatine strips in a bowl, cover with cold water and soak for 5 minutes, and then drain.

Discarding the bay leaf, purée the vegetables and juices in a blender and pass through a sieve. You should have about 3 cups of purée. Spoon some of this over the soaked gelatine and stir to dissolve, and then add this back into the rest of the purée. Stir in the tequila and the lime juice and add more salt if necessary. Divide the soup between six ½-cup ramekins or other little cups or bowls. Place in a dish or on a tray to make them easier to carry, and then cover and leave to cool. Chill in the fridge overnight. Serve with a teaspoon of crème fraîche or Greek yogurt in the center, and a few petals strewn over the top.

Vichyssoise

The reputation of this soup precedes it, and since it does boast luxurious ingredients, I guess it should be considered a treat. A variation is to make it with scallions (about 10 ounces), trimmed and sliced.

This soup is easily dressed up and especially good with a little smoked salmon, some shrimp or these crab toasts.

Serves 6

1 pound new potatoes,	½ cup white wine
peeled and roughly diced	3½ cups chicken stock
4 tablespoons unsalted butter	sea salt, white pepper
10 ounces leeks, (white portions only, sliced)	1 cup half and half
2 celery stalks, sliced	finely chopped chives, to serve

Bring a pan of salted water to a boil and cook the potatoes until tender. Drain and press them through a sieve. Melt the butter in a large saucepan and cook the leeks and celery over very low heat for 12–15 minutes, stirring frequently to prevent them from browning. Add the wine and cook for a few minutes to reduce it. Then add the chicken stock and some seasoning. Bring to a boil, and then cover and simmer over low heat for 20 minutes. Process the soup in a blender and add the puréed potato. Pass through a fine-mesh sieve, stir in the cream and taste for seasoning.

To serve hot, gently reheat the soup without boiling and ladle into warm bowls. Scatter some chives over each bowl and serve with the crab toasts (see below) if you wish. Alternatively, serve it lightly chilled.

On the side ## Crab toasts

Crab is a shellfish that can be prohibitively expensive. It is the brown meat that has the most flavor, something that European producers have long taken advantage of. You can find all kinds of well-priced seafood spreads online and in specialty markets, typically packaged in cans or tubes.

1 x 5-ounce tube of crab paste or spread,	a dash of Tabasco
e.g. Abba of Sweden	sea salt
6 tablespoons unsalted butter, softened	thin slices of baguette, toasted
a squeeze or two of fresh lemon juice	

Blend the crab paste, butter, lemon juice, Tabasco and a little salt in a food processor until smooth. Dollop onto slices of toasted baguette.

Leek and potato soup

This is a country cousin of *vichyssoise*, but without the cream you can settle down to a serious bowlful followed by another. I crave this soup whenever I am feeling below par, and am happy to live off it for many days at a time. There is something about the sweetness of the leeks with the comforting bite of the potatoes. The bacon is a garnish, and for the most part I am happy to pass on it, but it's good to know how to adorn your bowl of soup should you wish.

Serves 6

4 tablespoons unsalted butter
1½ pounds leeks (trimmed weight), sliced
1 large onion, peeled and chopped
⅔ cup white wine
6 cups fresh chicken or vegetable stock

6 ounces new potatoes, peeled and thinly sliced
sea salt, black pepper
To serve
½ pound bacon, diced
snipped chives

Melt the butter in a large saucepan over medium-low heat and cook the leeks and onion for 8–10 minutes until silky and soft, without browning, stirring occasionally. Add the wine and reduce until syrupy. Meanwhile, heat the stock to a boil in a separate pan. Add the sliced potatoes to the leeks and stir them around for a minute, then pour the boiling stock over the vegetables. Season and simmer for 8 minutes. At the same time, heat a dry frying pan over medium-low heat, add the bacon and cook for 7–8 minutes until dark and crisp, stirring occasionally. Remove with a slotted spoon to a plate lined with a paper towel and set aside to drain.

Blend the soup in batches in a food processor to a textured purée. Return to a clean saucepan, taste to check the seasoning and reheat gently. Ladle the soup into warm bowls, scatter some bacon and chives over the top and serve.

Potage parmentier

Asked on the spot to name a favorite food writer I am always at a loss, and then the answer or some thoughts on the subject trickle through in the hours that follow. "I meant to say Patricia Wells," I suddenly recall, a cooking author whose recipes are always superb and whose writing is beautifully evocative. Patricia Wells tells of her love of *potage parmentier* in her book *Bistro Cooking*. I'm not sure anyone else could convince me that a soup consisting of mainly potatoes, a couple of leeks and crème fraîche could be anything short of lacking – but it is every bit as good as she says.

Serves 6

1 pound new potatoes, peeled and
    roughly diced
2 good-sized leeks, trimmed and sliced

sea salt, black pepper
6 ounces crème fraîche
finely chopped tarragon or chervil, to serve

Place the vegetables, 1 quart of water and some seasoning in a medium saucepan. Bring to a boil, and then simmer over low heat for 30 minutes. Purée in a blender, return to the saucepan and stir in the crème fraîche. Reheat and serve scattered with the fresh herbs.

Chunky pea soup

Serves 4

5 tablespoons extra virgin olive oil, plus
   extra to serve
5 shallots, peeled, halved and thinly sliced
1 celery stalk, trimmed and thinly sliced
3 garlic cloves, peeled and finely chopped
5 leeks, trimmed, halved lengthways and
   thinly sliced

sea salt, black pepper
10 ounces fresh shelled peas
3 cups chicken stock
3 ounces pea shoots, coarsely chopped, plus a
   few extra shoots to serve
3 large handfuls of basil leaves

Heat 5 tablespoons of olive oil in a large saucepan over medium heat, add the shallots, celery and garlic and cook for 4–5 minutes until softened, stirring frequently. Add the leeks, season and cook for 4–5 minutes until glossy and soft, stirring occasionally. Stir in the peas, add the stock and bring to a boil, and then simmer for 5 minutes. Stir in the chopped pea shoots and cook for another minute.

Transfer half the soup to a food processor, add the basil and process into a textured purée, then stir this back into the pan with the rest of the soup. Taste for seasoning. Serve with a sprig of pea shoots in the middle of each bowl and plenty of olive oil drizzled over the top.

Ramson soup

Great for soothing frazzled nerves, this has lots of potato and a mass of chopped ramsons added at the end. The small white petals can be scattered over the soup, a little like chive flowers, for garnish. This is great made with watercress, arugula and pea shoots too.

Serves 4–6

4 tablespoons unsalted butter
4 medium onions, peeled and chopped quite finely
¾ cup white wine
1½ pounds new potatoes,
   peeled and roughly diced

5 cups chicken stock
sea salt, black pepper
7 ounces ramsons, plus a few flowers,
   (optional), to serve
crème fraîche (optional), to serve

Melt the butter in a large saucepan over medium-low heat, add the onions and cook for 6–7 minutes until softened, without browning. Add the wine, turn up the heat, bring to a boil and reduce by two-thirds. Add the potatoes, the chicken stock and some seasoning, and bring back to a boil. Turn the heat back down and simmer for 15 minutes or until the potatoes are tender when pierced with a knife. Using a potato masher, coarsely mash the potatoes into the soup. It needn't be completely smooth, small bites of potato are welcome. You can prepare the soup to this point in advance.

Just before eating, thinly slice the wild garlic and add it to the pan. Bring back to a boil and taste for seasoning. Ladle into warm soup bowls and serve immediately. You might like to drop a teaspoon of crème fraîche into the center of each bowl of steaming soup and scatter with a few wild garlic flowers if you have some.

This chunky pea soup makes the most of their comforting sweetness, with lots of pea shoots thrown in at the very end to provide a lively note. A little grated Parmesan would be very welcome here.

As you can't have failed to notice, I love texture in soups — something a little more challenging and interesting than a simple creamed soup, lovely as these are on occasions. This is especially true when soup is supper in itself, as it makes me feel as though I've eaten properly. Here not only do the broccoli stalks add to the soup's depth once they've been through the food processor, but the almonds bring a textured element to the party.

Broccoli and almond soup

Serves 6

1 pound broccoli
2 tablespoons unsalted butter
1 tablespoon extra virgin olive oil
1 large onion, peeled, halved and sliced
1 celery stalk, trimmed and sliced

2 ounces flaked almonds
6 cups chicken stock
½ cup white wine
sea salt, black pepper
crème fraîche (optional), to serve

Trim and finely slice the broccoli stalks, then cut up the florets. Heat the butter and oil in a large saucepan over medium heat, add the onion, celery, broccoli stalks and almonds and cook for 10 minutes, stirring occasionally, until softened and lightly browned. Meanwhile, bring the stock to a boil in a small saucepan.

Add the wine to the vegetables and cook until syrupy and reduced. Add the broccoli florets and stir for a moment until they darken, then pour in the stock, which should come back to a boil almost instantly. Season the soup and simmer for 5 minutes, and then purée it in a food processor. It should retain a slight texture, specked with the green of the broccoli. Taste for seasoning and serve in warm bowls with a spoon of crème fraîche in the center, if desired.

Fava bean soup with basil

In theory 5 ounces of bacon should suffice for this soup's crispy garnish, but as I find wandering fingers tend to get away with a considerable proportion before they hit the soup, 8 ounces is probably a better bet. Remember too that many packaged stocks contain considerable amounts of sodium so season at the end.

Serves 4

2 tablespoons unsalted butter
2 medium onions, peeled and chopped
2 garlic cloves, peeled and finely chopped
1 celery stalk, trimmed and sliced
½ cup white wine
2 pounds frozen fava beans
1 quart chicken or vegetable stock

2 large handfuls of basil leaves
sea salt, black pepper
To serve
5 ounces bacon, diced
crème fraîche (optional), to serve

Melt the butter in a medium saucepan over medium heat, add the onion, garlic and celery and cook gently for 8–10 minutes until softened and starting to brown. Add the wine and simmer until well-reduced and syrupy. Add the fava beans and the stock, bring to a boil and simmer for about 7 minutes. Purée the soup in batches with the basil, then pass it through a sieve back into a clean pan and taste for seasoning.

While the soup is cooking, gently fry the bacon in a dry pan over medium-low heat, stirring frequently until golden and crisp. Drain on a paper towel. Reheat the soup, and serve in warm bowls with a dollop of crème fraîche in the center if desired, and some bacon scattered over the top. Both the soup and the bacon can be made in advance.

Favorite tomato soup

This is a fresh take on the Campbell's classic, the soup so many of us crave, having been spoon-fed this velvety red soup, with a grilled cheese if we were lucky, when our mothers were too busy for anything else. For best results, go for cherry tomatoes on the vine, which are the sweetest and most intensely flavored tomatoes of all. But the real secret here is the celery salt, and it's well worth investing in a jar, although alternatively you could slice and sauté a couple of celery stalks with the onions.

Serves 6

4 tablespoons unsalted butter
2 medium onions, peeled and chopped
4 garlic cloves, peeled and finely chopped
3½ pounds ripe cherry tomatoes (or plum tomatoes, coarsely chopped)
½ cup heavy cream
¾ teaspoon sugar
sea salt
cayenne pepper
celery salt

Melt the butter in a large saucepan over medium-low heat and cook the onion for about 10 minutes until lightly golden, stirring occasionally. Add the garlic a couple of minutes before the end. Add the tomatoes and give them a quick stir, and then cover the pan with a lid and cook for 20–25 minutes until the tomatoes are soft and soupy, stirring halfway through.

Purée the soup in a blender and pass through a sieve. Return to a clean pan, add the cream, sugar and a little salt, and simmer gently for 15 minutes. Season with cayenne pepper and celery salt to taste.

Canned tomato soup

Andy Warhol turned Campbell's tomato soup cans into icons. When pressed for time try dressing up this go-to pantry classic:

~ *with a spoonful of fresh pesto*
~ *with a dollop of crème fraîche and some croutons*
~ *blended with some fresh basil*
~ *ladled over a slice of toast drizzled with olive oil and topped with plenty of chopped flat-leaf parsley*
~ *with lots of grated smoked Cheddar, such as Applewood*
~ *with little toasts piled with fried onions, sprinkled with grated Gruyère and grilled*
~ *with flakes of cooked smoked haddock and diced potato stirred in, topped with minced chives or flat-leaf parsley – an instant chowder*

Tomato cup-a-soup

This is for when you want a real, but instant, tomato soup. Drink it from mugs with a few croutons for a bit of crunch.

Serves 4–6

½ cup half and half
½ cup milk
1 medium onion, peeled and quartered
1 celery stalk, trimmed and sliced
1 medium carrot, trimmed, peeled and sliced
2 x 14-ounce cans of chopped tomatoes

1 tablespoon tomato ketchup
pinch of cayenne pepper
1 teaspoon cornstarch
1 heaping teaspoon sugar
sea salt
croutons (optional), to serve

Combine the half and half and milk in a medium saucepan. Process all the remaining ingredients in a blender and add to the pan. Bring to a boil and simmer for 15 minutes, stirring occasionally. Serve topped with croutons (see page 165) if desired.

Butternut squash soup with nutmeg and ginger

Butternut squash promises a more intense soup than pumpkin, and it tends to be my default when I am hovering between the two. But I do love experimenting with different types of squash, and enjoy buying pumpkin by the slice when I come across it sold in that manner. For this recipe the two are interchangeable.

Serves 6

Croutons
vegetable oil, for shallow-frying
3 thin slices of white bread, crusts removed, diced

Soup
4 tablespoons unsalted butter
1 large onion, peeled and chopped

2 tablespoons coarsely chopped fresh ginger
2 x 2-pound butternut squash, skinned, deseeded and coarsely chopped*
1 quart fresh vegetable or chicken stock
sea salt, black pepper
5½ ounces crème fraîche
freshly grated nutmeg

To make the croutons, heat a couple teaspoons of oil in a large pan over medium heat until a cube of bread is immersed in bubbles when added to the pan. Put in the bread cubes and fry until golden, stirring frequently. Remove, drain on two sheets of paper towels and leave to cool.

To make the soup, melt the butter in a large saucepan over medium heat, add the onion, ginger and squash and cook for about 5 minutes until glossy, stirring frequently. Add the stock and plenty of seasoning and bring to a boil, pressing the squash down with a spoon to submerge it. Simmer for 5–10 minutes until the squash is tender. Process the soup in batches in a blender along with the crème fraîche and a generous grating of nutmeg, then pass it through a sieve. Gently reheat, and serve with croutons scattered over the top.

* The simplest method here is to cut off a slice from the top and the bottom of the butternut squash and halve it where the bulb meets the trunk. Cut the skin off both sections, and then quarter, deseed and slice the bulb, and halve and slice the trunk.

Spinach soup with ricotta

A real pond green, not that I say that affectionately ever since a blanket of pond weed smothered my wild watercress, but it is a fabulous color, and the milky whiteness of the ricotta makes it even more dramatic. Gently warmed by the heat of the soup, the cheese is rendered exquisitely soft and creamy – in contrast to the crispness of the bacon.

Serves 4

4 tablespoons unsalted butter
3 medium onions (ideally white), peeled and chopped
sea salt, black pepper
½ cup white wine
1 quart chicken stock
18 ounces spinach leaves
3 ounces curly or flat-leaf parsley (leaves and fine stalks)
a squeeze of fresh lemon juice
To serve
8 strips bacon
4 tablespoons ricotta

Melt the butter in a large saucepan over medium-low heat, add the onions, sprinkle with a teaspoon of salt and cook for 15–20 minutes until soft and syrupy, stirring occasionally, without allowing them to brown. Add the wine, turn the heat up and cook to reduce it by half. Pour in the chicken stock and bring to a boil. Put in the spinach with half the parsley, bring back to a boil, and then cover and cook over a low heat for 10 minutes, stirring the soup after a couple of minutes to submerge the leaves. Add the remaining parsley at the last minute, and then purée the soup in a blender. Season with black pepper and a little more salt if necessary.

Gently reheat the soup, and add a squeeze of lemon juice – if this is added too far in advance the soup will dull in color.

While the soup is cooking, preheat the broiler and cook the bacon until golden and crisp.
Place a tablespoon of ricotta in the center of four warm soup bowls and ladle the soup around it. Lay a couple of strips of bacon in the middle and serve immediately.

Sweet corn and chile soup

Serves 6

2 tablespoons unsalted butter
2 tablespoons extra virgin olive oil
2 large onions, peeled and finely chopped
7 corn cobs
3 teaspoons finely chopped medium-hot
   red chile

1 quart vegetable stock
sea salt
2 tablespoons fresh lemon juice
5 tablespoons coarsely chopped flat-leaf parsley,
   plus extra to serve
sour cream (optional), to serve

Heat the butter and olive oil in a large saucepan over medium heat and cook the onion for about 10 minutes until nice and golden, stirring occasionally. Meanwhile, cut the kernels off the cobs using a sharp knife. Add these to the pan with the chile and cook for about 5 minutes, stirring occasionally. Add the stock and some salt, bring to a boil and simmer for 10 minutes until the corn is tender, but still crisp. Transfer two-thirds of the soup to a food processor and process into a coarse purée. Add this back to the pan and stir in the lemon juice and parsley. Taste for seasoning. Serve with a spoonful of sour cream if desired, and some more parsley scattered over the top.

Celery root and grainy mustard soup

Celery has a very distinctive flavor, that acquires an added dimension when combined with its relative celery root, which gives the soup a thick wholesome texture – whereas celery on its own is all water.

You could enrich the finished soup with some cream if you wish, or serve it with a swirl on top before scattering the bacon and pine nuts over the top.

Serves 6

6 tablespoons unsalted butter
2 leeks, trimmed and sliced
2 celery hearts, trimmed and sliced
   (inner leaves reserved)
2 pounds celery root, peeled and chopped
sea salt, white pepper

1 quart chicken or vegetable stock
1 teaspoon grainy mustard
To serve
5½ ounces bacon, diced
½ cup pine nuts

Melt the butter in a large saucepan over low heat. Add the leeks, celery and celery root, sprinkle with a heaping teaspoon of sea salt and cook very gently for 30 minutes, stirring frequently to prevent the vegetables from browning. Add the stock, bring to a boil and simmer over low heat for 15 minutes. Purée the soup in batches in a blender, and then pass through a sieve back into the pan. Whisk in the mustard and taste to check the seasoning.

At the same time, heat the bacon in a large pan over medium heat and fry in the rendered fat, stirring occasionally until golden and crisp. Add the pine nuts towards the end and fry for a couple of minutes. Drain on a couple layers of paper towel.

Gently reheat the soup and ladle into warm bowls. Scatter the bacon and pine nuts over the top and garnish with a few chopped celery leaves.

The idea of stripping kernels from a cob immediately evokes a time-consuming image, when in truth it takes no time at all — providing you do not let them shoot all over the kitchen worksurfaces and floor. The soup is true to its name, really sweet, but sharpened with a little lemon juice so it is well balanced.

Chunky carrot, saffron and cilantro soup

There is method in the apparent madness of this soup. Trust me that the end result is transformed by glazing the carrots first so that they take on an intense buttery sweetness, which is subsequently transferred to the saffron broth.

Serves 6

3 pounds large carrots, trimmed and peeled

3 shallots, peeled and finely chopped

4 cups chicken or vegetable stock

5 tablespoons unsalted butter, diced

large pinch of saffron filaments (about 30)

1 heaping teaspoon sea salt

1 heaping teaspoon sugar

5½ ounces crème fraîche

6 tablespoons chopped cilantro, plus a little extra to serve

Quarter the carrots lengthways and finely slice – you can do this with the slicing attachment of a food processor. Place them in a large saucepan with the shallots, ¾ cup stock, the butter, saffron, salt and sugar. Give everything a stir, bring the liquid to a simmer, and then cover and cook over medium heat for 8 minutes. Give the carrots another stir, turn up the heat and cook, uncovered, for 8–12 minutes, stirring towards the end to stop them from sticking to the pan. You will know when they are ready because the stock will have evaporated and the carrots will be glossy, coated in a buttery emulsion and meltingly tender.

Add the remaining stock and the crème fraîche and bring to a boil. Then stir in the chopped cilantro and season with more salt if necessary. Serve the soup in shallow bowls with the carrots piled in the center, and a sprinkle of cilantro over the top.

Cauliflower and cilantro soup

I am always amazed that with so few ingredients this soup can still pack such a punch, it's gorgeously aromatic, creamy white and silky. A cilantro purée, stirred through at the end, provides a dramatic finish.

Serves 4

2 tablespoons unsalted butter
1 onion, peeled and chopped
1 small cauliflower, cut into small florets
   (about 1½ pounds)
⅓ cup white wine

sea salt, white pepper
To serve
1 ounce cilantro leaves
3 tablespoons extra virgin olive oil
a squeeze of fresh lemon juice

Melt the butter in a large saucepan over medium-low heat. Add the onion, cauliflower and wine and cook for 10–15 minutes, stirring occasionally, until the cauliflower changes from a chalky white to a translucent white, without browning. Add 2⅓ cups water, plenty of salt and a little pepper. Bring to a boil, and then cover and cook over low heat for 15 minutes. Purée in a blender and return to the saucepan.

Meanwhile, process the cilantro, olive oil, lemon juice and a pinch of salt in a food processor into a purée. Serve the soup with a spoonful of the herb purée running through the soup's surface. Accompany with Skinny beef and Coleslaw (see below) if desired.

On the side
Skinny beef

1 x 1-ounce piece of beef tenderloin
extra virgin olive oil

sea salt, black pepper

Remove the beef from the fridge 20 minutes before cooking. Preheat a pan over medium-high heat. Brush the beef all over with oil and season. Sear the beef for 3–4 minutes on all four sides until it feels springy but soft, which will make it medium-rare. Place it on a rack set over a plate, loosely cover with foil and leave to cool, then wrap it in foil and refrigerate for at least an hour. Finely slice to serve.

Coleslaw

3 tablespoons sour cream
a couple of squeezes of fresh lemon juice
sea salt, cayenne pepper
⅛ onion
⅓ Savoy cabbage, heart only, finely sliced

1 narrow carrot, trimmed, peeled and finely sliced
   on the diagonal
¼ apple, cored and finely sliced
a handful of watercress
2 tablespoons walnut oil
1 ounce macadamia nuts

Blend the sour cream with a squeeze of lemon juice, a little salt and the juice from the onion, squeezing it with a garlic press. Arrange the cabbage, carrot, apple and watercress on a plate. Drizzle with the walnut oil and a squeeze of fresh lemon juice, and sprinkle with a little salt. Spoon the sour cream dressing over the top of the slaw, dust with cayenne pepper and scatter the macadamias over the top.

Two-pepper soup

A smooth, thick red soup with the warming heat of chile, and a little ginger. Chicken skewers and a broccoli salad turn it into a more substantial supper (see right).

Serves 4

4–5 tablespoons peanut oil

2 pounds sweet red peppers, core and seeds removed, coarsely chopped

2 medium onions, peeled and coarsely chopped

3 medium carrots, trimmed, peeled and sliced

1 celery heart, trimmed and sliced

3 garlic cloves, peeled and finely chopped

1 scant teaspoon finely chopped medium-hot red chile

1 teaspoon coarsely chopped fresh ginger

2 ripe tomatoes, halved

½ cup white wine

sea salt

pinch of sugar

4 pickled chiles, to serve

You will need to cook the peppers in batches. Heat a couple of tablespoons of oil in a large saucepan over medium heat, add half the peppers and cook for 8–10 minutes until lightly golden, glossy and softened, stirring occasionally. Transfer to a bowl while you cook the rest in the same way, adding another tablespoon of oil if necessary. Keep to one side.

Add another couple of tablespoons of oil to the pan, put in the onion, carrot and celery and cook for about 5 minutes until softened and starting to brown, stirring occasionally. Stir in the garlic, chile and ginger and cook for a few minutes to release their flavor. Add the tomatoes and the wine and cook until well-reduced. Add the peppers back to the pan, pour in 1½ cups water and season with a generous dose of salt and the sugar. Bring to a boil, and then cover and cook over low heat for 10 minutes. Process the soup in a blender and pass it through a sieve. Taste for seasoning. Ladle into warm bowls and serve with a pickled chile pepper in the center.

The Greengrocer

Chinese five-spice chicken skewers

Chinese five-spice is a great blend that calls for little else in a marinade for chicken. The smell as the spices hit the pan is tantalizingly good.

2 skinless free-range chicken breasts
peanut or vegetable oil
1 scant teaspoon Chinese five-spice powder
2 garlic cloves, peeled and crushed to a paste
1 medium red onion, peeled
sea salt, black pepper
lime wedges, to serve

Cut the chicken into 1 inch cubes and toss in a bowl with a tablespoon of oil, the Chinese five-spice powder and the garlic. Cover and chill for at least one hour. Cut the onion into chunks the same size as the chicken. Thread the onion and chicken a couple of pieces at a time onto eight 6–8 inch skewers.

Preheat a large pan over medium heat. Meanwhile, season the chicken skewers and drizzle with a little oil. Cook for about 2 minutes on all four sides until golden and firm. Brush a little oil over the lime wedges and briefly cook the flesh sides to brown them.

Grilled broccoli and sesame seed salad

1 pound tender-stem broccoli, trimmed
1 tablespoon sesame seeds
2 tablespoons peanut or vegetable oil
2 teaspoons sesame oil
sea salt, black pepper

Bring a large pot of salted water to a boil, add the broccoli and cook for 3 minutes. Drain into a colander and leave for a few minutes for the surface moisture to evaporate before transferring to a bowl. Toast the sesame seeds in a small pan over medium heat until lightly golden, stirring constantly, and then transfer to a plate and leave to cool.

Preheat a grill pan over medium heat. Blend the peanut and sesame oils together and drizzle over the broccoli. Season with salt and pepper and toss carefully. Grill the broccoli stems in two to three batches for 2–3 minutes on each side until golden, and then arrange on a plate. Scatter the sesame seeds over the top and serve warm or at room temperature.

White onion soup

This is in the *vichyssoise* league of heavyweight creamed soups. Pearly white onions have a particular character and finesse, and it's important to use them rather than yellow ones that are better reserved for French onion soup.

Serves 4–6

6 tablespoons unsalted butter
2 pounds white onions, peeled, halved and sliced
3 sprigs of thyme
sea salt, white pepper

½ cup white wine
2½ cups chicken stock
7 ounces crème fraîche
black pepper (optional), to serve

Melt the butter in a large saucepan over low heat. Add the onions and thyme, sprinkle with a heaping teaspoon of sea salt and cook for 30 minutes, stirring frequently to prevent the onions from browning. By the end they should be lusciously silky and soft. Pour in the wine, turn up the heat a little and simmer until it is well-reduced. Add the chicken stock, bring to a simmer and cook over low heat for 15 minutes.

Remove the thyme sprigs, and then purée the soup in a blender along with the crème fraîche and some white pepper. Taste to check the seasoning. Return to a clean saucepan and gently reheat. Serve in warmed soup bowls and season with black pepper, if desired.

Parsnip soup

Parsnips make for a fabulously aromatic soup, provided you balance their sweetness – a task performed here by the lemon juice. If you like creamy soups, you could add ½ cup heavy cream at the end, or swirl a tad over the top before serving. Another variation is the inclusion of a few rosemary or thyme sprigs along with the parsnips, removing them before you purée the soup. The bacon and pine nuts suggested for the Celery root and grainy mustard soup (see page 30) are equally good here. This is a good one for freezing.

Serves 6

4 tablespoons unsalted butter
2 medium onions, peeled and chopped
1 leek, trimmed and sliced
4 celery stalks, trimmed and sliced
2 garlic cloves, peeled and finely chopped

1½ pounds parsnips, trimmed, peeled, halved
    lengthways and sliced
juice of ½ lemon
1 quart chicken or vegetable stock
sea salt, black pepper

Melt the butter in a large saucepan over medium-low heat, add the onion, leek, celery and garlic and cook for 10–15 minutes, or until softened and glossy and just starting to brown, stirring occasionally. Add the parsnips and lemon juice and cook for 15 minutes, again stirring occasionally. Add the chicken or vegetable stock and some seasoning, bring to a boil and simmer for 10 minutes. Purée the soup in batches, and taste for seasoning. Serve in warmed bowls.

Beet and apple soup

Serves 6

5 tablespoons unsalted butter
2 medium onions, peeled and chopped
2 garlic cloves, peeled and finely chopped
1½ pounds raw beets, trimmed, peeled and sliced
2 apples, peeled, cored and sliced

¾ cup hard cider
5 cups chicken stock
sea salt, black pepper
3 bunches scallions, trimmed and sliced
3 tablespoons crème fraîche

Melt 4 tablespoons of butter in a large saucepan over medium-low heat and cook the onion and garlic for 5–8 minutes until soft and glossy, stirring occasionally. Add the beets and apples and continue to cook for another 5 minutes, again stirring occasionally. Add the cider and reduce until syrupy, and then add the chicken stock and some seasoning. Bring to a boil over high heat, and then cover and simmer over low heat for 30 minutes. Purée the soup in batches in a food processor. Return it to the saucepan and taste to check the seasoning.

About 10 minutes before the soup is ready, heat the remaining tablespoon of butter in a pan and cook the scallions over low heat until soft, about 8 minutes, seasoning them and stirring frequently.

Reheat the soup if necessary before ladling it into warm bowls. To serve, place a spoonful of the scallions in the center and a heaping teaspoon of crème fraîche on top. Serve immediately.

Green minestrone with mint and almond pesto

A mass of lovely late spring veggies with a mint purée coursing through the broth, this immediately evokes everything you associate with spring. Minestrone is something to be played with – basil could replace the mint and parsley, and pine nuts the almonds, which will make for a more traditional soup.

Serves 4

8 tablespoons extra virgin olive oil, plus extra
    to serve
1 celery heart, trimmed and sliced
2 leeks, trimmed and sliced
2 garlic cloves, peeled and finely chopped
6 ounces green beans, ends trimmed, cut into
    ½-inch pieces
6 ounces fresh or frozen baby fava beans

6 ounces fresh or frozen peas
2¾ cups vegetable stock
sea salt, black pepper
2–3 handfuls of spinach leaves
1 ounce mint leaves
1 ounce flat-leaf parsley leaves
1 ounce slivered almonds
3 ounces freshly grated Parmesan cheese

Heat 3 tablespoons of oil in a large saucepan over medium-low heat, add the celery and leeks and cook for 6–8 minutes until glossy and softened, stirring occasionally. Add the garlic just before the end. Stir in the green beans, fava beans and peas, and then add the stock and seasoning. Bring to a boil and simmer for 5 minutes. Add the spinach and cook for 1 minute, stirring to submerge the leaves. Process half the soup in a food processor into a textured purée, and then stir it back in with the rest of the soup.

Process the mint, parsley and almonds with 5 tablespoons of oil in a food processor, and then add the Parmesan and briefly blend again. Stir into the hot soup right at the end and serve with a drizzle of oil.

The sweet tartness of apple brings out the flavor of beets. It's not a vegetable that everyone likes, it's like it or loathe it, people rarely sit on the fence with this one. But if you know you are among like-minded beet lovers, this is a great soup.

Double mushroom soup

This is everything I love in a mushroom soup – hearty and rustic, thick and meaty. Mushrooms are so full of juice, they make great soup material. Any kind will be good here, but the combination of crimini and shiitake is particularly tasty, saving you the expense of wild varities.

Serves 4

5 tablespoons extra virgin olive oil, plus extra to serve
2 tablespoons unsalted butter
4 ounces bacon, diced
4 shallots, peeled, halved and sliced
1 tablespoon rosemary needles
3 garlic cloves, peeled and finely chopped
1 large new potato (about 7 ounces), peeled and diced
⅓ cup white wine
14 ounces crimini mushrooms, trimmed and sliced
7 ounces shiitake mushrooms, trimmed and sliced
3 cups chicken or vegetable stock
¼ teaspoon dried red pepper flakes
sea salt
To serve
5 ounces shiitake mushrooms, trimmed and sliced
coarsely chopped flat-leaf parsley

Heat a tablespoon of oil and the butter in a large saucepan over medium heat, add the bacon and cook for 4–5 minutes until it starts to brown. Add the shallot and rosemary and cook for 3 minutes, stirring in the garlic towards the end. Stir in the potato, add the wine and simmer until well-reduced and syrupy.

You will need to cook the mushrooms in batches. Heat a tablespoon of oil in a large pan over high heat. Add about a third of the mushrooms and cook for a few minutes, stirring frequently, until golden. Set aside on a plate while you cook the rest in the same manner.

Add the cooked mushrooms to the saucepan, along with the stock, the red pepper flakes and some salt. Bring to a boil and simmer for 10 minutes. Process the soup in batches in a food processor and return to the pan.

To serve, heat a tablespoon of oil in a large pan, add the remaining 5 ounces shiitake mushrooms, season with salt and sauté for several minutes until softened and golden. Ladle the soup into warm bowls, scatter with the shiitake mushrooms and sprinkle with plenty of parsley and a little drizzle of olive oil.

The Dairy

A few croutons with molten Stilton or Camembert, grilled Cheddar sandwiches, some feta stirred into a soup at the end, instantly create that comforting yummy factor that we're seeking. Or it might be a little cheese crumbled into the bowl before ladling the soup on top. It's a great way of using up the ends of a slice of cheese, the darkened Stilton or hardened Parmesean rind, that if anything has more flavor than the cheese it once held within. Such raw materials bought from a good cheese shop will be a world apart from the unloved cheese from a supermarket. The ins and outs of storing various cheeses, which will depend on their type and their age, is highly specialized. I also appreciate such purveyors for their wide assortments of cream, yogurt and fromage frais, often ladled from a large tub into a smaller one on demand. There is every reason to hope such products will have just as much character as the cheeses they are next to, all of which promise rich velvety soups with bright textures. Here you are also more likely to find products with their full complement of fat, which goes hand in hand with flavor.

Russian cherry soup

Fruit soups are an eccentricity, strikingly whimsical, and I'm not entirely sure that I can take them seriously, but the Russians do and so do the Georgians. With their enviable harvest of sour cherries, what better way of serving them than in a soup, or is it simply that fiercely cold winters drive you to frivolity with the arrival of summer?

Any scepticism I guess is mainly that they fall outside the usual repertoire – where do the cheeseboard and salad fit in? But therein lies the answer, they fill a gap that other soups can't. Fruit soups are at home at either end of a meal and they are a fine way of preceding a spicy main course, not always an easy find. Flaky little Grecian pastries are a flight of fancy, but the singularly salty character of feta and halloumi go very well together.

Serves 4

3 ounces dried cherries
1-inch cinnamon stick
1 clove

3-inch strip of orange zest (removed with a
    vegetable peeler)
½ bottle (375ml) sweet white wine
juice of 1 orange, strained

Place all the ingredients in a medium saucepan with 1½ cups water. Bring to a simmer, and then cover and cook over low heat for 30 minutes. Discard the orange zest and remove the spices. Leave to cool. Strain the soup through a fine mesh sieve, reserving about half of the cherries as a garnish. Cover and chill. Serve the soup in small bowls with a few cherries scattered on top, accompanied by the cheese pastries (see below) if desired. You can also serve this soup warm.

On the side

White cheese pastries

3 ounces feta, crumbled
3 ounces halloumi, grated
1 ounce pine nuts
1 tablespoon chopped mint

freshly grated nutmeg
1 medium egg, beaten
7 ounces filo pastry sheets
4 tablespoons unsalted butter, melted

Preheat the oven to 400°F. To make the filling, combine the feta and halloumi with the pine nuts, mint, some freshly grated nutmeg and the egg in a bowl.

Paint a sheet of filo pastry with a little melted butter and lay another sheet on top. Cut into rectangular strips about 3 inches by 7 inches. Place a heaping teaspoon of the filling near the top of one of the strips, fold in one of the long sides by a ½ inch, and then fold the top corner down over the filling to form a triangle. Paint the surface with a little more melted butter, and fold the pastry over and over again and again, painting the surface with each turn, until you have a small triangular package. Place this on a baking sheet, and repeat with the remaining ingredients.

Liberally paint any unbuttered surfaces with butter and bake the pastries for 20 minutes until deep golden brown. Serve warm.

Pear and Stilton soup

Many years ago I spent New Year's in a secluded, rented house overlooking the beach. While the setting was spectacular, it gave new meaning to the expression "bare essentials" in the way that only vacation homes of a certain ilk can achieve. I still remember every mouthful of the Stilton soup that we ate one evening, by far the most comforting aspect of the trip. A rich golden turkey stock is a great match for this cheese soup, and the pears complement it discreetly without being obvious. You could serve it in little shot glasses if you're catering for a larger group, or simply in a mixture of small coffee cups, in which case it will feed many more than suggested.

Serves 4–6

4 tablespoons unsalted butter
1 celery heart, trimmed and sliced
3 medium carrots, trimmed, peeled and sliced
2 leeks, trimmed and sliced
2 pears, peeled, cored and chopped
½ cup white wine
3 cups chicken or turkey stock

sea salt, black pepper
5½ ounces Stilton, crumbled
To serve
crème fraîche
cocktail shortbreads (see page 167) or
*   sliced baguette*

Melt the butter in a large saucepan over medium heat, add the celery, carrot and leeks and cook very gently for 8–10 minutes until glossy and softened, stirring occasionally. Add the pears and stir, then add the wine and simmer until well-reduced. Add the stock and season lightly (bear in mind the salty Stilton is going to be added). Bring to a boil, and then cover and cook over low heat for 10 minutes. Stir in the Stilton, cover, remove from the heat and leave to stand for a few minutes to allow the cheese to melt. Purée the soup in batches in a blender, and then pass through a sieve. Adjust the seasoning. Serve with a little crème fraîche dolloped in the center, accompanied by cocktail shortbreads (see page 167) or sliced baguette.

Curried eggplant soup

Eggplant soup may seem odd, but that lovely succulence melts down beautifully into some chicken stock with some spices. Here the heat is pleasantly tempered by a refreshing raita.

Serves 4

6 tablespoons peanut oil
2 medium eggplant, cut into a ½-inch dice
3 garlic cloves, peeled and finely chopped
1-inch piece of fresh ginger, peeled and
  finely chopped
1 medium-hot red chile, seeds removed,
  finely sliced
½ teaspoon turmeric

1 teaspoon ground coriander
1 teaspoon ground cumin
1 quart chicken stock
sea salt
2 level teaspoons sugar
1 tablespoon lemon juice
4 tablespoons finely chopped cilantro
warm pitas (optional), to serve

You will need to cook the eggplant in batches. Heat 2 tablespoons oil in a large non-stick pan over medium heat, add half the eggplant and cook for 7–8 minutes until soft and golden, stirring occasionally. Transfer to a bowl and repeat with the remaining eggplant.

Heat 2 tablespoons oil in a medium saucepan over medium heat, add the garlic, ginger and chile and cook for a couple of minutes until softened and fragrant. Add the spices and stir, then add half the cooked eggplant, the chicken stock, 2 teaspoons of salt and the sugar. Bring to a boil and simmer for about 8 minutes. Process the soup in a blender, return to the pan and stir in the reserved eggplant. Gently reheat, and then stir in the lemon juice and fresh cilantro. Adjust the seasoning and serve in warm bowls. Accompany with cucumber raita (see below) and warm pitas, if desired.

On the side ## Raita

Prepare this in advance of the soup.

½ cucumber, peeled
7 ounces fromage frais
½ teaspoon finely chopped medium-hot
  jalapeño

pinch of sugar
sea salt
1 scallion, trimmed and finely sliced

Coarsely grate the cucumber and, using your hands, squeeze out as much liquid as possible. In a bowl, stir the grated cucumber into the fromage frais. Add the jalepeño, sugar and a little salt to taste. Transfer to a clean serving bowl and scatter the scallions over the top. You can make this up to a couple of hours in advance, in which case cover and set aside in a cool place.

Beet and pomegranate soup

Our fondness for beets pickled in vinegar is no coincidence. It is a root that relishes tart ingredients, and the most successful beet soups play to this attribute – an apple in there, or a little orange juice makes all the difference. Here, though, the role is fulfilled by the pomegranate, ever an artful balance of sweet and sour, it brings out the best in this curious vegetable. Their matching vermilion hues are also rather stunning.

Serves 6

4 tablespoons unsalted butter
2 medium onions, peeled and chopped
1½ pounds raw beets, trimmed, peeled and sliced
2 garlic cloves, peeled and finely chopped
¾ cup pomegranate juice

5 cups chicken stock
sea salt, black pepper
freshly grated nutmeg
2 ounces pine nuts
pomegranate syrup (optional), to serve

Melt the butter in a large saucepan over medium-low heat and cook the onion for 5–8 minutes until soft and glossy, stirring occasionally. Add the beets and garlic and continue to cook for another 5 minutes, again stirring occasionally. Add the pomegranate juice and reduce until syrupy, then add the chicken stock, some seasoning and a little grated nutmeg. Bring to a boil, and then cover and simmer over low heat for 30 minutes.

Meanwhile, preheat the oven to 400°F. Spread the pine nuts over the base of a small baking dish and toast for 8–9 minutes until lightly golden, then remove and leave to cool. Purée the soup in a blender, and then return it to the saucepan and taste to check the seasoning. Serve the soup in warm bowls with a drizzle of pomegranate syrup, if desired, and a few pine nuts scattered on top. It can also be accompanied with the Grilled goat cheese sandwiches (see below).

On the side

Grilled goat cheese sandwiches

These are a petit complement to the soup. You may want to double the recipe so everyone gets their own.

6 thin slices of white bread, cut from a small loaf
3½ ounces thinly sliced hard goat cheese

extra virgin olive oil
3 small handfuls alfalfa sprouts, to serve

Make three sandwiches with the bread and sliced cheese. Heat a large pan (ideally non-stick) over high heat for a couple of minutes, or two pans if necessary. Add a little oil to the pan, and then add the sandwiches. Turn the heat down to medium-low and cook gently for 3–5 minutes on each side until golden on the outside and oozing melted cheese. Gently pry each one apart and fill with the sprouts, then close and cut into quarters or fingers.

Watercress soup

I love those diminutive, light introductions to finer lunches, and this soup is definitely a candidate for that. However it is the little grilled Cheddar sandwiches here that turns this into a complete meal starring a cheese that typically doesn't get enough respect.

Serves 4–6

4½ cups chicken or vegetable stock
4 tablespoons unsalted butter
9 ounces watercress (3 good-sized bunches), leaves and fine stalks
10 ounces new potatoes, peeled and finely sliced
sea salt, black pepper
1 ounce flat-leaf parsley, leaves and fine stalks
crème fraîche or sour cream, to serve

Bring the stock to a boil in a small saucepan. Melt the butter in a large saucepan over medium heat, add the watercress and stir until it wilts. Add the potato slices and cook for a minute, then pour in the boiling stock and add some seasoning. Simmer the soup for 6 minutes, then process it in a blender with the parsley. Season to taste and serve with a dollop of crème fraîche or sour cream, accompanied by the grilled sandwiches, if desired (see below).

On the side

Grilled Cheddar sandwiches

unsalted butter for spreading
8 thin slices of white bread, cut from a small loaf
5½ ounces grated sharp Cheddar
Dijon mustard

Butter the slices of bread on one side. Pair them into sandwiches with the cheese on the inside and the butter on the outside, spreading one of the unbuttered sides in the middle with mustard. These can be made in advance, in which case cover and refrigerate them.

To grill the sandwiches, heat a large pan (preferably non-stick) over high heat for several minutes. Add as many sandwiches as will fit, turn the heat down to medium-low and cook for 4–5 minutes on each side, or until golden and the cheese has melted. Prepare the rest in the same manner. Cut into little squares or triangles to serve.

A classic and personal favorite. The large handful of flat-leaf parsley at the end adds freshness and the promise of a leprechaun Irish green color.

Celery soup with Camembert and tarragon butter

This is a soup I've actually made while in France, where fine Camembert and tarragon are found everywhere. As for the bread, it need not necessarily be the finest baguette – a day-old or slightly burnt loaf from the patisserie will do. Look for the basket labelled *"pain au soupe."*

Serves 4

3 tablespoons unsalted butter
1 head of celery, trimmed with outer stalks discarded, thinly sliced
2 leeks, outer layers discarded, thinly sliced
¾ cup white wine
5 cups chicken stock
sea salt, black pepper

Toasts
4 slices of baguette, ½-inch thick
3 ounces Camembert, sliced
Tarragon butter
4 tablespoons unsalted butter
1 heaping tablespoon fresh, chopped tarragon

Melt the butter for the soup in a large saucepan over medium-low heat and cook the celery and leeks for 8–10 minutes until glossy and soft, stirring occasionally without allowing them to brown. Add the wine and reduce by half, then add the chicken stock and some seasoning. Bring to a simmer and cook over low heat for 25 minutes.

Meanwhile, preheat the oven to 400°F. Lay the slices of baguette on a baking sheet and toast for 7–8 minutes until lightly golden. Remove and leave to cool, and then lay the sliced cheese on top.

To serve, place the toasts back in the oven for 5 minutes until the cheese is melted but still retains its shape. Meanwhile, melt the remaining butter in a saucepan and add the chopped tarragon. Place one of the cheese toasts in each base of four warmed shallow soup bowls and ladle the soup on top. Drizzle with tarragon butter and serve immediately.

Leafy green soup with feta and olives

Serves 4

4 tablespoons unsalted butter

1 celery heart, trimmed and thinly sliced

1 leek, trimmed and thinly sliced

1 bunch of scallions (about 6), trimmed
    and sliced

5 cups vegetable or chicken stock

sea salt, black pepper

2 ripe tomatoes, cores removed, chopped

3 ounces watercress, coarsely chopped

1½ ounces arugula, coarsely chopped

5½ ounces feta, crumbled

3½ ounces pitted black olives, coarsely chopped

extra virgin olive oil, to serve

Melt the butter in a large saucepan over medium heat. Add the celery, leek and scallions and cook gently for about 2 minutes until glossy and just softened. Pour in the stock, season and bring to a boil, then simmer over low heat for 15 minutes.

Add the tomatoes, watercress and arugula, and then turn up the heat slightly and simmer for 2 minutes. Stir in the feta and black olives and remove from the heat. Taste for seasoning and serve in warm bowls, drizzled with extra virgin olive oil.

Cauliflower cheese soup

Cauliflower has always skirted the fringes of popularity, though I'm not quite sure what it could have done to deserve this. I guess some people might be put off by its texture, and this might explain why we so often smother it in silky cheese sauce. Obviously its texture doesn't apply to soup, where its subtle elegant aroma is at the core, but I'd like to think doubters could be converted here. The cheese sauce is such a great marriage and it happily translates into a soup.

Serves 4

2 pounds cauliflower florets (about 1 large
    cauliflower)

2 tablespoons unsalted butter

¼ cup all-purpose flour

2 cups chicken or vegetable stock

1 cup milk

⅓ cup heavy cream

sea salt, black pepper

1 bay leaf

3½ ounces grated sharp Cheddar

1 teaspoon Dijon mustard

1 teaspoon grainy mustard

freshly grated nutmeg, to serve

Bring a large pot of salted water to a boil, add the cauliflower and simmer for 10 minutes or until it is really tender. Drain into a colander.

Meanwhile, melt the butter in a medium non-stick saucepan, stir in the flour and cook for about 1 minute, or until the roux is well-integrated. Remove from the heat, gradually whisk in the stock, milk and cream. Season and add the bay leaf. Bring to a boil, stirring constantly, and then simmer over low heat for 10 minutes. Discard the bay leaf and stir in the Cheddar and the mustards.

Process the soup base with the cauliflower in batches in a blender, then return it to a clean saucepan. Reheat gently to serve, adjust the seasoning and serve with a dash of freshly ground nutmeg.

A soup with a spring in its step, courtesy of lots of chopped watercress and arugula. The feta and black olives stirred in at the end ensure a really lively bowlful, brimming with goodness.

Sweet potato and cumin soup with feta yogurt

Sweet potatoes are fabulous soup material, in fact I think this is my favorite way of serving them. Like parsnips and carrots, the result is thick and comforting. All three vegetables can be approached in a similar manner, so if you have a particular preference for one it may translate well in this recipe – they all marry well with spices and salty cheeses. Here it's the orange-fleshed potatoes you want.

Serves 6

3 tablespoons extra virgin olive oil
1 large onion, peeled and chopped
4 garlic cloves, peeled and finely chopped
1 heaping teaspoon ground cumin
a pinch of dried red pepper flakes
2¼ pounds sweet potatoes, peeled and
 thickly sliced

5 cups chicken or vegetable stock
sea salt
3 ounces feta, crumbled
5½ ounces Greek yogurt
2 tablespoons finely chopped sun-dried tomatoes
 (optional), to serve

Heat the oil in a large saucepan over medium heat. Add the onion and cook for a few minutes until soft and glossy, stirring occasionally. Add the garlic, cumin and red pepper flakes and cook for a minute longer. Add the sweet potato, and continue to cook for another couple of minutes, stirring frequently. Pour in the stock and season with salt, bring to a boil and simmer over low heat for 20 minutes, by which time the potato should be very tender. Purée the soup in batches in the blender. Return it to the saucepan and season with a little more salt, if necessary.

Combine the feta and yogurt in a bowl and dollop a spoonful on top of each bowl of soup. Scatter a teaspoon of chopped sun-dried tomatoes on top, if using.

The Dairy

Chilled cucumber and cilantro soup

There should be a definite bite of jalepeño in this soup to challenge the cucumber – go for a large chile that will provide flavor as well as heat. The salmon roe can be subsituted with crabmeat or shrimp.

Serves 4

To serve

½ cucumber, peeled and finely sliced

1 rounded teaspoon sea salt

1 rounded teaspoon sugar

4 heaping teaspoons salmon roe

Soup

1 x 16-ounce container of plain yogurt

1 x 6-ounce container of Greek yogurt

½ cucumber, peeled and roughly cut into pieces

1 heaping teaspoon chopped fresh jalapeño

½-inch piece of fresh ginger, peeled
and chopped

2 handfuls of cilantro leaves

1 heaping teaspoon sea salt

1 rounded teaspoon sugar

Toss the finely sliced cucumber with the salt and sugar in a bowl and set aside for 30 minutes to draw out the juices. Drain the cucumber into a sieve, rinse thoroughly in cold water to get rid of the salt and sugar, and then drain again. Pat dry on paper towels or on a clean dish towel and set aside in a bowl.

To make the soup, place all the ingredients in a blender and process until smooth and creamy. Taste and add more salt or sugar, if necessary.

Pour the soup into bowls and float some of the cucumber slices on the surface. Scatter a heaping teaspoon of roe over the cucumber slices, using your fingers to break it up, and serve immediately.

Chilled spinach and yogurt soup

Lovely dark leaves that go down with a thick, creamy yogurt spiked with cumin. I'd eat this soup with some warm bread, green olives, and perhaps a pickle.

Serves 6

6 tablespoons extra virgin olive oil,
plus extra to serve

18 ounces baby spinach

3 shallots, peeled and finely chopped

4 garlic cloves, peeled and crushed to a paste

1 heaping teaspoon cumin

sea salt, black pepper

1 x 16-ounce container of plain yogurt

You will need to cook the spinach in about four batches. Heat a tablespoon of oil in a large pan over medium heat, add a quarter of the spinach and cook, stirring, until it wilts. Transfer to a bowl and cook the remaining spinach in the same manner, then coarsely chop it on a cutting board.

Heat a couple of tablespoons of oil in a large saucepan over medium heat and cook the shallots for several minutes until softened and lightly golden. Add the garlic and cumin, and then add the spinach and plenty of seasoning. Stir again. Add 1¾ cups water and bring to a boil, then stir in the yogurt. Pour into a bowl and leave to cool completely. You can either eat it at room temperature, or cover and chill for a couple of hours in the fridge. Serve with a drizzle of extra virgin olive oil.

Warming chicken and rice soup

A package of chicken drumsticks is the starting point here (or drumsticks and thighs if that's how they come). Not only do they provide a basic stock but succulent little shreds of meat.

Cooking with yogurt comes with a rule – when it forms the base of a hot soup it needs to be stabilized to prevent it from splitting. Here it is combined with egg yolk and flour before heating through, but even then it is best to avoid boiling it. This is quite a hearty soup, so it's main course material.

Serves 6

4 tablespoons extra virgin olive oil
sea salt, black pepper
8 free-range chicken drumsticks or thighs
1 medium onion, peeled and finely chopped
5 garlic cloves, peeled and finely chopped
6 tablespoons finely chopped mint

2 ounces basmati rice
2 medium egg yolks
1 heaping teaspoon plain flour
1 x 16-ounce container of Greek yogurt
paprika (optional), to serve

Heat a couple of tablespoons of olive oil in a large saucepan over medium heat, season the drumsticks and brown them on all sides. Add 3 cups water, bring to a boil and then cover and simmer over low heat for 30 minutes. Meanwhile, place the rice in a bowl, cover with plenty of cold water and leave to soak for 30 minutes, then drain. Transfer the cooked drumsticks to a bowl, reserving the stock in the pan. Leave the chicken until cool enough to handle, and then remove the meat from the bones and dice.

Heat the remaining olive oil in a medium saucepan over medium heat and cook the onion for about 5 minutes until lightly golden, stirring occasionally. Stir in the garlic and half the mint and cook for a minute until fragrant, then add the rice and stir until coated in the oil. Skim off any excess fat from the chicken stock, and then add it to the pan. Bring to a boil, cover and simmer over low heat for 12–15 minutes until the rice is just tender.

Meanwhile, whisk the egg yolks with the flour in a small bowl. Whisk in about a tablespoon of the Greek yogurt, and then stir the mixture back into the yogurt.

Add the diced chicken to the soup and heat through. Whisk a ladleful of the hot soup into the yogurt to thin it, and then stir this back into the soup. Turn the heat up a little so that the soup is almost boiling – until the odd bubble breaks the surface – and then stir in the rest of the mint and taste for seasoning. Serve in warm bowls, with a dusting of paprika, if desired.

Curried coconut yogurt soup

This soup tastes richer than the ingredients suggest, which is due to the yogurt base. It is derived from the Indian restaurant Zaika in London, where they have a truly enlightened approach to Indian cooking, which can so often be heavy. I particularly love the little crunchy black mustard seeds in all that milky sweetness. As always, the chicken brochettes on the side are optional, but delicious – you could always double up and have them with a salad to follow.

Serves 4

8 ounces plain yogurt
¾ ounce chickpea flour, sifted
1¼ cups chicken stock or water
2 tablespoons vegetable oil
2 teaspoons black mustard seeds
1-inch piece of fresh ginger, peeled and
*   finely chopped*

1 garlic clove, peeled and thinly sliced
1 jalapeño, seeds removed, sliced
3 whole red chiles
1 x 14-ounce can of coconut milk
sea salt
2 tablespoons finely chopped cilantro
1 tablespoon unsalted butter, to serve

In a large bowl, blend the yogurt and chickpea flour with the chicken stock or water and whisk until smooth. Heat the oil in a medium saucepan, add the mustard seeds and once these fizzle add the ginger, garlic, and all of the chiles. Stir to combine, and then add the yogurt and chickpea flour mixture. Bring to a boil, stirring. Add the coconut milk, season the soup generously with salt and return to a boil. Simmer for a couple of minutes. Strain the soup through a sieve into a bowl and return it to the pan.

Gently reheat the soup, stir in the fresh cilantro and serve in warm cups or bowls with a pat of butter in the center, accompanied by the chicken brochettes, if desired (see right).

Chicken brochettes

1 teaspoon chopped red chile, seeds removed
1 teaspoon cumin seeds
1 teaspoon coriander seeds
1 teaspoon finely chopped cilantro
juice of ½ lemon

1 tablespoon vegetable oil
sea salt
2 skinless free-range chicken breasts,
   cut into 1-inch dice

Heat the chile, cumin and coriander seeds in a small pan until they release their aroma, and then grind the mixture in an electric grinder (or grind well in a mortar and pestle). Transfer to a bowl and add the fresh cilantro, lemon juice, vegetable oil and a little salt. Add the chicken and coat it with the spice mixture, and then leave to marinate while you prepare the soup.

Thread the chicken onto four 8-inch metal skewers or soaked bamboo ones. Heat a large pan or grill pan over medium-high heat, and cook the chicken on all sides for about 7 minutes in total.

Parsley soup with saffron cream

Serves 4

a pinch of saffron (about 20 threads)
2 tablespoons unsalted butter
2 medium onions, peeled and chopped
2 large bunches (about 8 ounces total) flat-leaf parsley (stalks and leaves), ends trimmed

2 tablespoons basmati rice
1 quart vegetable stock or water
sea salt, black pepper
2 tablespoons crème fraîche

Infuse the saffron threads in a teaspoon of boiling water. Melt the butter in a medium saucepan over medium heat and cook the onions and the parsley stalks for a few minutes until softened.

Add the rice and the vegetable stock or water and bring to a boil. Simmer for about 15 minutes, adding the parsley leaves a few minutes before the end. Process in a blender and season to taste, then ladle into warm bowls. Blend the saffron water with the crème fraîche and serve a spoonful over the top.

Spring vegetable soup with yogurt

The vegetables will be at their brightest green when the soup is freshly made, as the acidity in the yogurt will cause them to dull in color. Use the list as a guide and include whatever vegetables you happen to have, providing they are spring-like and green – asparagus, sugar snaps and fava beans all come to mind.

Serves 4

2 medium egg yolks
1 heaping teaspoon plain flour
1 x 16-ounce container of Greek yogurt
3 cups vegetable or chicken stock
sea salt, black pepper
7 ounces broccoli florets, trimmed and roughly chopped

4 ounces snow peas, trimmed, and then roughly chopped
10 ounces fresh or frozen peas
3 scallions, trimmed and sliced
1 tablespoon chopped tarragon
4 tablespoons chopped flat-leaf parsley
2 ounces slivered almonds (optional), to serve*

Whisk the egg yolks with the flour in a small bowl, and then whisk in a tablespoon of the Greek yogurt. Stir this mixture back into the tub of yogurt.

Bring the stock to a boil in a medium saucepan and season it. Add the broccoli and cook for 3 minutes, then add the snow peas, peas and scallions and cook for another 3–4 minutes or until the vegetables are tender. If using frozen peas, cook them separately to avoid losing the boiling point.

Whisk a little of the soup broth into the yogurt mixture, and then stir this back into the soup and heat almost to boiling point – until a bubble or two breaks the surface. Stir in the herbs. Process the soup in batches in a food processor so that it still retains a bit of texture. Adjust the seasoning and serve sprinkled with slivered almonds, if desired.

* To toast almonds, arrange them in a thin layer on a baking sheet and bake for 7–8 minutes at 400°F.

A really simple parsley soup, which demonstrates just how much of this herb you can get away with including without it becoming overpowering. The more you add the cleaner and more refreshing the soup seems to become.

Butternut squash soup with truffle cream

In northern Italy entire restaurants are devoted to truffles, where every single dish permeates their scent. Black winter truffles (*Tuber melanosporum*), summer truffles (*Tuber aestivum*) and white ones (*Tuber magnatum*) are used in minute quantities to cast an intoxicating cloak over pasta and risottos, a plate of raw beef or a cheese fondue. Once familiar with their scent it is easy enough to understand the Italians' passion for them, and also their sky-high price, being as rare as they are. Summer truffles are the most common, and they are the ones we usually encounter here, preserved whole in small jars, but you occasionally see the black winter truffles too – albeit at a price. We can tap into the scent of the white ones courtesy of tiny bottles of pungent truffle-flavored oil, a few drops of which will leave you with the lingering suggestion of it long after you have finished the last mouthful. Like most ingredients in this league, there is no need for a host of other flavors or complication, the scent is so magnificent it says it all.

The soup relies on a potato masher rather than a blender, so it's on the rustic side, and that smooth little spoonful of cream makes all the difference. You may like to serve some crisp fried croutons with the soup (see page 165).

Serves 4

4 tablespoons unsalted butter

7 ounces bacon, diced

3 leeks, trimmed and sliced

2 x 2-pound butternut squash, skinned, seeded and coarsely diced (about 2 pounds of flesh once the skin and seeds are removed)

½ cup white wine

5 cups chicken stock

sea salt, black pepper

½ cup sour cream

1 teaspoon truffle oil

Melt the butter in a large saucepan over medium heat, add the bacon and cook for 6–8 minutes until lightly colored and starting to crisp, stirring occasionally. Add the leeks and sauté for about 5 minutes until soft and translucent, and just starting to brown. Add the butternut squash and cook for 10 minutes over low heat, again stirring occasionally. Pour in the wine and simmer until syrupy and well-reduced. Now add the chicken stock and season with black pepper and a little salt, bearing in mind the bacon will add saltiness to the dish as well. Bring to a boil and simmer for 20 minutes. Using a potato masher, mash the butternut squash until you have a thick purée. Adjust the seasoning.

Blend the sour cream and truffle oil in a small bowl. Serve the soup in warm bowls with the truffle cream spooned in a swirl and with a scattering of croutons on top, if desired (see page 165).

The Fishmonger

For many of us, our first taste of the Mediterranean is inextricably linked to our first taste of "soupe de poisson," that rich, thick golden soup that we might otherwise have turned our nose up at were it not for the crisp slices of baguette, the intoxicating rust-colored rouille and grated Gruyère that melted into it effortlessly. It left us with a sense of taking our first step into an adult world, as did a bowl of "moules marinière." I find it heartening how young children will take to working their way through a pile of these black mollusks, relishing the hands-on ritual, justification for getting seriously messy. Even now, I find fish soups have a sense of being special, they're celebratory, regardless of how humble the fish.

White vegetable soup with smoked haddock

Here fish serves as the star topping rather than the soup's base allowing a little fish to stretch a long way – a silky smooth cauliflower and turnip soup topped with salty, buttery flakes of smoked haddock. If you want to omit the crème fraîche for a lighter soup, then increase the chicken stock by about $\frac{1}{3}$ cup.

Serves 6

2 tablespoons unsalted butter
1 head of cauliflower, cut into small florets
2 large turnips, peeled and diced
2 medium onions, peeled and chopped
3 cups chicken stock
sea salt, white pepper
3½ ounces crème fraîche
freshly grated nutmeg

To serve

14 ounces undyed smoked haddock fillet
   (or smoked trout or smoked sturgeon)
2 tablespoons unsalted butter (plus an extra
   2 tablespoons if prepping soup in advance)
1 bay leaf
a squeeze of fresh lemon juice
1 tablespoon minced chives

Melt the butter in a large saucepan over low heat and cook the cauliflower, turnip and onion for about 20 minutes, stirring occasionally, until glossy but without allowing them to brown. Add the stock and some seasoning, bring to a boil, and then cover and cook over low heat for 15 minutes. Purée the soup in batches in a blender with the crème fraîche. Season with nutmeg, and more salt and pepper, if necessary.

Cut the smoked haddock to fit the base of a medium saucepan. Add a few teaspoons of water, dot with 2 tablespoons butter and add the bay leaf. Bring to a boil, cover and cook over low heat for 5 minutes. Transfer the fish to a plate and coarsely flake, discarding the skin. The soup and fish can be prepared to this point a few hours in advance, in which case cover and set aside in a cool place.

When you are ready to serve, reheat the soup. Melt 2 tablespoons of butter in a small saucepan, add the flaked haddock and gently reheat. Season with a squeeze of lemon juice and stir in the chives. Ladle the soup into bowls and serve with the haddock in the center.

Crab and fennel soup

For convenience I usually buy my crab pre-cooked and picked-over fresh from the Fishmonger or in a can.

Serves 6

3–4 tablespoons extra virgin olive oil
3 fennel bulbs (about 2 pounds), trimmed
    and chopped
3 celery stalks, sliced
3 narrow carrots, trimmed, peeled and sliced
½ cup white wine

1 quart fish stock
zest of 1 lemon, plus a couple of squeezes of juice
sea salt
9 ounces white crabmeat
cayenne pepper
½ cup heavy cream, whipped

Heat 3 tablespoons of oil in a large saucepan over medium heat, add half the vegetables and cook for 8–10 minutes until soft and translucent, stirring occasionally. Transfer these to a bowl and cook the remainder in the same way, adding a little more oil to the pan if necessary. Return all the vegetables to the pan. Add the wine and simmer until well-reduced. Add the stock, lemon zest and some salt, bring to a boil, and then cover and simmer for 20 minutes.

Process the soup in batches in a blender, pass it through a sieve, and then return it to the saucepan. Place the crabmeat in a bowl, pour in some of the hot soup and mix with a spoon, then stir this back into the rest of the soup. Season to taste with lemon juice, salt and cayenne pepper, and reheat gently without boiling. To serve, place a spoonful of cream in the bottom of six bowls and ladle the hot soup on top.

Cream of carrot soup with grilled scallops

Like the white vegetable *velouté* on page 72, where the fish is a garnish, here a few scallops provide a royal touch to a humble carrot soup – although it is well-served with a simple sprinkle of parsley or chives.

Serves 6

1 quart chicken stock
2 pounds large carrots, trimmed, peeled
    and sliced
10½ ounces crème fraîche
sea salt, black pepper

½ teaspoon sugar
To serve
6 medium scallops (about 7 ounces)
peanut or vegetable oil
a squeeze of fresh lemon juice

Bring the stock to a boil in a large saucepan. Add the carrots, bring back to a boil, and then cover and simmer over low heat for 15 minutes. Purée the soup in batches in a blender, along with the crème fraîche, a generous pinch of salt, a grinding of pepper and the sugar.

Gently reheat the soup to serve. Rinse the scallops in fresh, cold water. Slice each scallop lengthwise into two or three discs. Heat a large, non-stick or cast-iron pan over high heat. Brush the scallops with oil, seasoning just one side, and grill for 30 seconds on each side. It's easiest to do this in two batches. Squeeze a little lemon juice over the top. Ladle the soup into bowls and serve with the scallops in the center.

Pea soup with squid

Richard Olney's recipe for squid stuffed with peas in *Ten Vineyard Lunches* (to be picked up should you ever come across it in a used bookstore) has been a defining moment for me – I have never wanted to eat this cephalopod any other way since first cooking the dish, although this soup is rather basic. For anyone averse to the slightly slippery textures that characterize particular foods, the solution lies in combining them with their opposite, and this combination of squid with peas is a match made in heaven. Other duos that work well together include shellfish with lentils or coarsely crushed potatoes, and oysters with sourdough bread and unsalted butter. Here the sweet, satisfying texture of the peas is just right with the squid, and balances out that slippery tendency that in the wrong company can be off-putting.

Serves 4

10½ ounces squid, prepared
2½ cups fish stock
3 tablespoons extra virgin olive oil
1 large onion, peeled and chopped
½ cup dry vermouth
2 cups fresh shelled peas

1 teaspoon sugar
sea salt, black pepper
10 good-sized basil leaves
½ pound raw peeled jumbo shrimp
a squeeze of fresh lemon juice
2 tablespoons coarsely chopped flat-leaf parsley

Carefully rinse the squid with cool water on all sides, dry with paper towels and slice into fine rings.

Bring the fish stock to a boil in a small saucepan. Heat 2 tablespoons olive oil in a large saucepan over medium heat, add the onion and cook for 5–6 minutes until softened and just starting to brown, stirring occasionally. Add the dry vermouth and cook until it is syrupy. Add the peas and stir, then add the boiling stock, the sugar and some seasoning. Bring back to a boil and simmer for 5–6 minutes or until the peas are tender.

Pour the soup into a food processor, add the basil leaves and blend to a coarse purée – the soup should still retain some texture. Adjust the seasoning, it may need more salt, and then return it to the saucepan and reheat gently.

At the same time, heat a tablespoon of olive oil in a large pan over high heat. Add the shrimp and sauté for 1 minute, and then add the squid rings and cook for 1 minute more. Season, squeeze with a little lemon juice and toss in the parsley. Serve the soup in warm bowls with the squid and shrimp spooned into the center.

Smoked haddock and potato chowder

One of those classic combinations that is just as successful in an omelette as it is in chowder. Because this does not require fish stock, it is a great stew to have up your sleeve. The technique is to cook the bacon and leeks in one pan, and the haddock, buttermilk and cream in another and then combine them at the very end. This ensures perfect results without splitting the milk, which can be a risk when everything is cooked together.

Serves 4

2 tablespoons unsalted butter
7 strips of bacon, cut into ½-inch strips
3 leeks, trimmed and sliced
1½ cups buttermilk
¾ cup heavy cream
1 pound new potatoes,
*   peeled and cut into ½-inch dice*

1 bay leaf
1 pound undyed smoked haddock fillet
*   (or smoked trout or smoked sturgeon),*
*   skinned and cut into 1-inch pieces*
black pepper
coarsely chopped flat-leaf parsley, to serve

Melt the butter in a large saucepan over medium heat, add the bacon and cook for 7–9 minutes, stirring occasionally to separate the pieces, until it is lightly browned. Add the leeks and continue to cook for about 7 minutes until softened and just starting to brown.

Meanwhile, bring the buttermilk and cream to a boil in another large pan with the potatoes and bay leaf, and simmer over low heat for about 8 minutes. Add the haddock and poach for 5 minutes until the potatoes are tender and the haddock flakes. Combine the contents of the two saucepans and season with black pepper. Serve in warm soup bowls, sprinkle with parsley.

Variation ## Seabass and mussel chowder

Traditional New England chowder is served with oyster crackers, and it may be that you have access to the authentic item, but saltines do a fine job crumbled over the top. You could just as well use clams instead mussels, although the latter tend to be much easier to come by – partially due to the industry's successful attempts at farming them – and they always promise lots of saline juices, which stand in as a stock in a soup.

Place *18 ounces cleaned mussels* (see page 78) in a large saucepan, cover and cook over high heat for about 4 minutes until they open. Leave the pan half-covered with the lid until the mussels are cool enough to handle, and then shell them, reserving the broth – you should have a little under ½ cup.

Combine the mussel broth with the buttermilk and cream, and replace the haddock with sea bass, skinned and cut into 1- to 2-inch pieces. Stir the shelled mussels into the cream base to heat through at the end. Serve scattered with *coarsely crumbled saltines* as well as parsley.

Garlic butter mussels

One of my favorite starters in small seafood restaurants is a platter of mussels sizzling in a pool of garlicky butter. This recipe couldn't be simpler – you dot the cooked mussels with garlic butter, cover with a lid and leave it to melt.

Serves 6

6 tablespoons unsalted butter
3 garlic cloves, peeled and crushed to a paste
juice of ½ lemon
a dash of Tabasco
5 tablespoons finely chopped flat-leaf parsley

7 pounds cleaned mussels (see below)
3 shallots, peeled and finely chopped
½ cup dry white wine
a baguette and unsalted butter, to serve

To make the garlic butter, place the butter, garlic, lemon juice and Tabasco in the bowl of a food processor and process until creamy and amalgamated. Add the chopped parsley and give another quick whirl to mix it in. Do not worry if a little of the lemon juice seeps out, most of it will have been incorporated. Transfer the butter to a bowl.

Place the mussels with the shallots and wine in a large, heavy-bottomed pot, and cover with a tight-fitting lid. Heat the pan over a high heat for about 5 minutes, stirring halfway through, by which time the mussels should have just steamed open. Dot the garlic butter over the mussels, put on the lid and leave for a few minutes, then give them a stir. Accompany with bread and butter.

Variation

More stew than soup...

Strain the mussel juices into a large bowl, reserving the cooked mussels in the pan. Pour the juices into a clean pan, discarding the last little gritty bit of liquid, and boil over high heat to reduce by half. Meanwhile, dot the mussels with garlic butter, cover with a lid and leave to melt. Pour the reduced juices back over the mussels to serve.

* Give the mussels a good wash in a sink of cold water, discarding any that are broken or that do not close when tapped. Pull off any beards and scrape off any barnacles. If they are very dirty, give them a second rinse.

Provençal red mullet soup

With many fish there are other types that can stand in, but red mullet stands on its own, with its meaty texture and hint of oiliness that is in no way permeant – as much as I love mackerel and salmon, they leave others to understand that you're no doubt getting your full complement of Omega 3. Mullet also has a uniquely rich flavor and soft, buttery skin. The main downside are the row of bones running down the center of each fillet, no problem for restaurants where deboning fish is second nature, but here where only small pieces are called for, the solution lies in cutting either side and remove the bones as a long, thin strip. A generous dollop of rich buttercup-yellow mayonnaise, and we're transported to the south of France.

Serves 6

3–4 tablespoons extra virgin olive oil, plus extra to serve

2 large onions, peeled, halved and sliced

2 fennel bulbs, trimmed and chopped

6 garlic cloves, peeled and smashed

2½ pounds ripe plum tomatoes, quartered

a pinch of dried red pepper flakes

2 strips of orange zest, removed with a vegetable peeler

½ cup white vermouth

1 quart fish stock

sea salt, black pepper

5½ ounces baby spinach leaves

1½ pounds red mullet fillets, cut into 2-inch pieces

6 thick slices of day-old, coarse-textured white bread, e.g. ciabatta

2½ ounces oily black olives, pitted and halved

Saffron mayonnaise

1 medium egg yolk

1 teaspoon Dijon mustard

sea salt

1 cup peanut oil

a pinch of saffron (about 20 threads), ground and infused with 1 teaspoon boiling water for 10 minutes

a squeeze of fresh lemon juice

First prepare the soup base. As you're going to be straining this, the vegetables don't have to be perfectly diced. Heat the olive oil in a large saucepan over medium-high heat, add the onion, fennel and garlic and cook, stirring occasionally, for 8–10 minutes until softened and starting to brown. Add the tomatoes, chili flakes, orange zest, vermouth, fish stock and a generous dose of salt. Bring to a boil, and then cover and cook over low heat for 45 minutes. Pass through a sieve into a large bowl, pressing out as much of the juice from the vegetables as possible. Taste for seasoning. The soup can be made up to this point a day in advance, in which case cover and leave to cool, and then chill in the fridge.

To make the saffron mayonnaise, whisk the egg yolk, Dijon mustard and a little salt together in a medium bowl. Very gradually whisk in the peanut oil, to begin with just a few drops at a time, and then once the mayonnaise has started to emulsify add in a more generous stream. Stir in the saffron liquid halfway through, when the mayonnaise seems too thick to whisk, and then continue whisking in the rest of the oil. Season with a squeeze of lemon juice. Store, covered, in the fridge and bring back to room temperature before eating.

Shortly before serving, bring the soup to a boil in a large saucepan or heavy-bottomed pot. Stir in the spinach and cook for about a minute. Season the fish with salt and pepper and add to the soup. Bring back to a boil over medium-high heat, and then simmer for 1 minute. Toast the bread, place one piece in the base of six warm, shallow soup bowls and drizzle with olive oil. Ladle in the soup, and serve with a dollop of saffron mayonnaise and a few olives scattered over the top.

Mussel soup with tomato and chile

This soup is one of a favorite trio of mussel stews – the hint of chile with the tomato and mussel juices is especially satisfying, and for those of us in northern climes makes for a great warm weather soup to be eaten outside on a summer's evening.

Serves 4

6 pounds cleaned mussels (see page 78)
½ cup white wine
3 garlic cloves, peeled
3 tablespoons extra virgin olive oil, plus extra to serve
4 tablespoons chopped flat-leaf parsley
1 x 14-ounce can of chopped tomatoes
1 small dried red chile, finely chopped
4 slices of baguette, ½-inch thick

Place the mussels in a large saucepan with the wine. Cover with a lid and cook over high heat for 5 minutes, by which time they should have opened. Transfer them to a bowl, and pour the cooking juices into a separate bowl, discarding the gritty bit at the bottom. Depending on how energetic you're feeling, you may like to shell half the mussels.

Finely chop two of the garlic cloves. Heat the olive oil in a large saucepan over medium heat, add the chopped garlic and half the parsley and allow to sizzle momentarily until the garlic just begins to brown, then add the tomatoes and chile. Turn the heat down and cook very gently for about 15 minutes, stirring occasionally, until the oil rises to the surface and separates out from the tomatoes. The soup can be prepared to this point in advance.

To serve, add the mussel juices to the tomato base and heat together, then add the mussels to the pan. Cover and reheat for a couple of minutes, stirring once. Toast the slices of bread, and then give each one a quick rub with the reserved garlic clove. Place these garlicky croutons in the base of four soup bowls, drizzle with a little olive oil, and then ladle the soup over the top. Sprinke with the remaining parsley and drizzle with another splash of olive oil.

Curried smoked haddock and potato stew

This comes close to a chowder but, without any bacon, curry spices partner up with the haddock instead. You could also look beyond India to a Middle Eastern spice blend, providing it isn't too hot. Alternatively, stir in some chopped watercress or flat-leaf parsley at the end, or simply relish its rich creaminess with a warm crusty roll.

Serves 6

2 cups buttermilk
1 cup heavy cream
1 pound new potatoes, peeled and cut
  into a ½-inch dice
1 bay leaf
1 pound undyed smoked haddock fillet
  (or smoked trout or smoked sturgeon),
  skinned and cut into 1½-inch pieces

4 tablespoons unsalted butter
3 leeks, trimmed and sliced
1 celery heart, trimmed and thinly sliced
3 carrots, trimmed, peeled and thinly sliced
2 teaspoons mild curry powder
sea salt, black pepper
a squeeze of fresh lemon juice

Bring the buttermilk and cream to a boil in a large pot with the potatoes and bay leaf, and simmer over low heat for about 8 minutes. Add the haddock and poach for another 5–6 minutes or until the potatoes are tender and the haddock flakes.

At the same time, melt the butter in a large saucepan over medium heat, add the leeks, celery and carrot and cook for about 7 minutes until soft and just starting to brown, then stir in the curry powder. Combine the contents of the two saucepans and season with salt and pepper and a generous squeeze of fresh lemon juice. Serve in warm soup bowls.

Moules marinière

Moules marinière is one of the greatest fish stews/soups, awesome in its simplicity. The small seaside cafés along the Cotentin Peninsula in France use the small, orange *moules de bouchot* farmed in the tidal waters along the coast on wooden stakes. This particular recipe stems from a favorite and very eccentric little café perched on top of the dunes at Blainville-sur-Mer, called La Cale, meaning "the slipway."

Serves 2

3 tablespoons peanut or vegetable oil
2 tablespoons very finely chopped onion
2 tablespoons very finely chopped shallot
1 garlic clove, peeled and finely chopped
⅓ cup white wine

4 pounds cleaned mussels (see page 78)
3 ounces crème fraîche
a handful of coarsely chopped flat-leaf parsley
sourdough bread and unsalted butter, to serve

Heat the oil in a large saucepan over high heat, add the onion, shallot and garlic and cook for about a minute until softened. Add the wine and simmer to reduce by half. Add the mussels, cover with a lid and cook for 5–6 minutes until opened. Stir in the crème fraîche and parsley and serve with sourdough bread and butter.

A chowder pie

Chowders transport us to some silvered jetty in Maine fringed with pastel clapboard houses, where we can dangle our legs in the cool blue water, or so we wish. The word itself is supposed to be derived from the French *chaudière* and thought to have been introduced to Newfoundland by Breton fishermen, possibly inspired by their own tradition of *cotriade* that includes potatoes.

We can't always recreate exact dishes, especially when it comes to fish stew. A chowder, however, is easier than most. Traditionally it contains salt pork fatback (which for many will most closely translate to bacon), fish or shellfish of many descriptions, often thickened either with flour or potatoes and some milk. Either way chowder is generous in spirit, and here the essential milkiness is added as a spoonful of cream at the very end.

Serves 4

2 tablespoons unsalted butter

6 strips bacon, cut into thin strips

3½ ounces baby leeks or scallions, trimmed and thickly sliced

3½ ounces baby carrots, trimmed, peeled and thickly sliced on the diagonal

3½ ounces broccoli (florets and tender stems), thickly sliced

3½ ounces sugar snap peas, ends trimmed and halved

1¾ cups chicken stock

7 ounces undyed smoked haddock fillet, skinned and cut into a ½-inch dice

5½ ounces raw, peeled shrimp

4 tablespoons coarsely chopped flat-leaf parsley

sea salt, black pepper

1 x 13-ounce package of prepared puff pastry

1 egg yolk blended with 1 tablespoon milk

crème fraîche, to serve

Preheat the oven to 400°F. Melt the butter in a large saucepan over medium heat, add the bacon and cook for 7–9 minutes, stirring occasionally to separate the pieces, until it is lightly browned. Add the vegetables and continue to cook for another couple of minutes, then remove the pan from the heat.

Add the chicken stock, smoked haddock, shrimp, parsley and a little seasoning and stir gently to combine. Divide the soup between four 1–1½ cup ovenproof bowls or ramekins.

Roll out the pastry a little thinner than it is on a lightly-floured worksurface, and cut out four shapes ½-inch bigger than the top of each bowl or ramekin. Brush the rim of each pastry shape with egg wash and place it painted-side down on top of each dish, pressing down carefully around the sides. Cut a couple of small slits in the pastry at opposite sides of each bowl, just inside the rim, and brush with egg wash. Place the bowls inside a roasting pan and bake for 20 minutes. Serve the crème fraîche separately, leaving each diner to cut into the pastry and dollop a spoonful into the soup.

Bourride

I used to make this with monkfish, before it was known to be endangered, but these days I find red snapper is a good choice. I tend to leave the skin on, which is not unpleasant to eat, as it helps hold the morsels together. Any other firm-fleshed, white fish will be good – seabass for example – and shellfish are a welcome addition too.

Serves 4

Aioli
2 medium egg yolks
6 garlic cloves, peeled and crushed to a paste
sea salt
¼ cup extra virgin olive oil
¼ cup peanut oil
1 teaspoon fresh lemon juice
Croutons
extra virgin olive oil, for shallow frying
12 slices of baguette, ½-inch thick
1 garlic clove, peeled
Soup
1½ cups fish stock
½ cup white wine

2 shallots, peeled and finely chopped
1 leek, trimmed and sliced
1 fennel bulb, trimmed and diced
1 strip of orange zest, removed with a vegetable peeler
a bouquet garni of a bay leaf and a few thyme and parsley sprigs, tied with string
sea salt, black pepper
1½ pounds red snapper fillets, cut into ½-inch pieces
a pinch of saffron (about 20 threads), ground and infused with 1 tablespoon boiling water
coarsely chopped flat-leaf parsley, to serve

To make the aioli, whisk the eggs yolks, crushed garlic and a pinch of salt together in a large bowl. Gradually whisk in the oils, a few drops at a time to begin with until the mayonnaise takes, and then in a continuous stream. Stir in the lemon juice at the end.

To make the croutons, heat a few drops of oil in a large pan over medium heat until it is hot enough to surround a slice of bread with bubbles. Fry the slices of baguette until lightly golden – crisp at the edges but soft in the middle. Rub each one with the garlic clove.

Place the stock, wine, vegetables, orange zest, bouquet garni and seasoning in a large saucepan and bring to a boil. Cover and simmer for 10 minutes. Season the fish with salt and add to the pan, return to a simmer and cook, covered, for about 3 minutes until the fish is firm. Using a slotted spoon, transfer the fish and vegetables to a warm serving dish or bowls, discarding the herbs and peel. Add the saffron infusion to the pan. Pour the broth into the aioli, whisking to blend. Return to the pan and gently heat until slightly thickened, without boiling. Strain the broth over the fish and vegetables, sprinkle with chopped parsley and accompany with the croutons.

This is second to bouillabaisse in the hall of fame of Provençal fish soups or stews, although it travels more readily, the key to its character being the aioli used to thicken the broth. And it is truly luxurious, a gorgeous ivory broth with prize morsels of fish.

Normandy fish soup

This is the classic fish soup that is served in nearly all of Normandy's seaside restaurants. This recipe is based on Jean-Christophe Chavaillard's *soupe de poisson* served at his restaurant Le Cap a L'Ouest overlooking the bay of Mont Saint Michel – a rich aromatic golden soup, dished up with croutons, *rouille* and grated Gruyère, it makes for a sustaining meal. Such soup is often sold in large jars and exported, but these packaged soups have little of the character of the real thing. However the difficulty in making it lies with the selection of fish normally used, a large pile of turbot, sole bones, conger eel and small swimming crabs known as *etrilles*. And then of course you need a mixer with industrial strength to break down the shells and bones when it is puréed. So this is a home-friendly take on it, shell-on shrimp can replace the brown crab meat, and you can substitute other fish for the squid, if they are not available. This soup is inevitably quite a lot of work, but it can be made in advance and also freezes well.

Serves 6–8

6 tablespoons extra virgin olive oil
4 shallots, peeled and coarsely chopped
3 celery stalks, sliced
1 fennel bulb, trimmed and chopped
1 leek, trimmed, halved lengthways and sliced
2 carrots, trimmed, peeled and sliced
1½ pounds very ripe tomatoes, quartered
4 garlic cloves, peeled and sliced
2 ounces parsley, coarsely chopped
1 x 750ml bottle of white wine
14 ounces sea bass fillets, cut into ½-inch pieces
14 ounces brown crabmeat

1 pound squid (cleaned weight), or hake fillets, cut into ½-inch pieces
6 cups fish stock
3 ounces tomato paste, plus 1 tablespoon
1 small dried red chile, crumbled
½ teaspoon mild curry powder
paprika
sea salt, black pepper
1 teaspoon unsalted butter blended with 1 teaspoon plain flour
crème fraîche, thin slices of toasted baguette, finely grated Gruyère and rouille (see page 92), to serve

Heat the olive oil in a large saucepan over medium heat and cook the shallots, celery, fennel, leek and carrot for 10–15 minutes until lightly golden, stirring occasionally. Add the tomatoes, garlic and parsley and continue to cook for 10–12 minutes until really soft, stirring occasionally. Add the white wine, bring to a boil and cook over a medium-high heat to reduce by about three-quarters.

Add all the seafood, fish stock, 3 ounces tomato paste, the chile, curry powder, a little paprika and some seasoning. Bring to a boil and simmer over low heat for 20 minutes, skimming the suface foam when necessary. Process the soup in batches in a blender and press through a sieve. Return the soup to the pan, stir in the remaining tablespoon of tomato paste to give the soup some color. Add the butter and flour paste in small pieces and simmer until melted.

Serve in warm bowls with a spoon of crème fraîche, if desired, accompanied by the croutons, Gruyère and *rouille* – first spread the crouton with *rouille*, pile on some Gruyère and float in the soup.

A simple bouillabaisse

When we think of fish soup, more often than not we think of *bouillabaise*, which of all the regional fish soups along the Mediterranean is the one that is most celebrated. Few of us, however, will ever have actually eaten an authentic Marseillaise *bouillabaise*, something I regard as a positive rather than a negative; it is a dish that perfectly illustrates regionality or the special characteristics acquired when it is produced within a specified area.

You can only experience a true *bouillabaise* in the area of Marseille, and even then given the depletion of local fish stocks, it will probably continue to evolve further over the years from its starting point centuries ago as a poor fisherman's make-do supper, using the least valuable of the day's catch boiled up in a pot of seawater. Whatever the subsequent inclusion of tomatoes, saffron and other aromatics, it traditionally contains three fish specific to the region.

The most famed of these, and the most elusive is scorpion fish, a bony specimen that I have never even found in Normandy, a haven for fish cooks and hardly a million miles away. Conger eel and searobin perhaps. The other defining features of a *bouillabaise* are the serving of the broth separately from the fish, with croutons and *rouille*, a spicy garlic fest of a sauce, and particular aromatics that we associate with Provence – fennel, saffron, thyme, bay and often orange is used to scent the soup.

Any fish soup should be approached on the basis of what is available locally and sustainably-sourced, and in the United States (or elsewhere in the world) that calls for a broad interpretation of the fish included. I am also inclined to dish up a single, hearty bowl of soup rather than to separate out the fish from the broth, not least because to be authentic the fish would be cooked unfilleted and overcooked by the time it had flavored the broth. Filleted fish, which takes no more than minutes to cook through, is surely preferable. So the starting point is to cheat with a good ready-made fish stock and from there you want the interest provided by several different types of fish, but pretty much any selection of filleted fish will be fine. You need 2½ pounds in total which is a fair quantity, so I'd suggest using farmed fish as part of the line up.

Serves 6

4 tablespoons extra virgin olive oil
2 large onions, peeled, halved and sliced
2 fennel bulbs, trimmed and chopped
6 garlic cloves, peeled and smashed
2 pounds ripe plum tomatoes, quartered
a pinch of dried red pepper flakes
a good pinch of saffron (about 20 threads)
a few parsley stalks
a few sprigs of thyme
1 strip of orange zest, removed with a
    vegetable peeler

⅓ cup white wine
1 quart fish stock
sea salt, black pepper
18 ounces new potatoes, scrubbed or peeled as
    necessary
7 ounces scallops
18 ounces cod fillets, skinned and central bones
    cut out, cut into 1-inch pieces
18 ounces seabass fillets, skinned and central
    bones cut out, cut into 1-inch pieces
thin slices toasted baguette, to serve

continued on the next page

Heat the olive oil in a large saucepan over medium-high heat, add the onion, fennel and garlic and cook, stirring occasionally, for 8–10 minutes until softened and starting to brown. Add the tomatoes, red pepper flakes, saffron, parsley, thyme, orange zest, wine, fish stock and a generous dose of salt. Bring to a boil, cover and cook over low heat for 45 minutes, then pass through a sieve, pressing out as much of the juice from the vegetables as possible. Taste for seasoning. The soup can be made up to this point a day in advance.

Up to an hour or two before serving, bring a large pot of salted water to a boil and cook the potatoes for 15–20 minutes until tender, then drain them into a colander. Halve the scallop meats into two discs and reserve with the other fish pieces. Cover and chill until required.

Shortly before serving, bring the soup to a boil in a large cast-iron dutch oven, season the fish with salt and pepper and add to the soup with the potatoes. Bring back to a boil over medium-high heat and simmer for 2 minutes. Ladle the soup into warm bowls and accompany with croutons and the *rouille*.

On the side ## Rouille

Despite its North African derivation, harissa is exactly what *rouille* or "rust" calls for. Another shortcut here is to buy red peppers in a jar rather than roasting your own.

½-ounce day-old white bread (weight without crusts)
½ red pepper, roasted, skinned and deseeded
2 garlic cloves, peeled
1 teaspoon harissa
1 large egg yolk

1⅓ cups extra virgin olive oil
1⅓ cups peanut oil
a pinch of saffron (about 20 threads), ground and infused with 1 tablespoon boiling water
fresh lemon juice
sea salt

Place the bread, red pepper, garlic and harissa in a food processor and reduce to a paste. Add the egg yolk, then trickle in the oils in a thin stream as though making a mayonnaise. Stir in the saffron liquid and season with lemon juice and salt.

Romesco de peix

This Catalan fish stew owes its deliciously sweet and aromatic nature to the *romesco* used to thicken it. A red pepper sauce, made with ground nuts, here it thickens the fish broth in the same way that an aioli is used in France, but the result is gutsier and altogether more rustic. I used to make this using monkfish instead of the sea bass suggested, which is more traditional, but conscience and a little rationale suggest that the stew will be just as good using a less-threatened species. Should you have access to any small clams, these can be included as well as, or instead of, the mussels.

Serves 4

12 whole, skinned almonds
1 slice of white bread
4 tablespoons extra virgin olive oil,
*   plus extra for brushing*
4 ripe tomatoes, halved
3 garlic cloves, peeled
1 teaspoon sweet paprika
a pinch of saffron (about 20 threads)
1 teaspoon sherry vinegar

½ cup white wine
1 large onion, peeled and chopped
2 red peppers, cored, seeds and membranes
*   removed, thinly sliced*
1 cup fish stock
18 ounces sea bass fillets, skinned and cut into
*   1-inch pieces*
sea salt, black pepper
18 ounces cleaned mussels (see page 78)

Preheat the oven to 400°F, lay the almonds out in a small baking sheet and toast for 10 minutes. Meanwhile, preheat a grill pan over medium heat for about 5 minutes. Brush the bread on both sides with olive oil and toast on the grill pan until golden. Remove and set aside. Now brush the tomatoes with oil and grill them too, cut-side down first, and then the skin side for several minutes until striped with gold and softened. Remove from the pan, set aside on a plate and peel off the skins once cool enough to handle.

Break up the toasted bread, place it in the bowl of a food processor and process into crumbs. Add the almonds and pulverise, then transfer to a bowl and set aside. To make the *romesco* sauce, place the garlic, tomatoes, paprika, saffron, vinegar and wine in the food processor and process into a smooth sauce.

Heat the olive oil in a large saucepan over medium heat, add the onion and sauté for 5 minutes until transluscent. Add the peppers and sauté for another 10 minutes until the onions are golden and the peppers have softened. Add the *romesco* sauce and the fish stock and bring to a boil. Simmer over low heat for 20 minutes, stirring occasionally.

To serve, stir the almond breadcrumbs into the simmering soup. Season the sea bass with salt and pepper and add to the pan with the mussels. Bring to a boil, and then cover and cook over high heat for 5 minutes. Taste for seasoning and ladle into warmed soup bowls.

More Asian than Mediterranean. Just as you might eat a small bowl
of rice and vegetables with miso soup, here a little addition of
egg-fried rice is the sideshow to a light saffron broth and grilled salmon.

Salmon and saffron broth

Serves 4

a pinch of saffron (about 20 threads)
2 tablespoons peanut oil, plus extra
    for brushing
1 shallot, peeled and finely chopped
½ cup dry white vermouth

2 cups fish stock
sea salt, black pepper
14 ounces salmon fillet, skin on
7 ounces baby spinach
lemon or lime quarters, to serve

Grind the saffron in a pestle and mortar and infuse for 30 minutes in a tablespoon of boiling water.

Heat a tablespoon of oil in a medium saucepan over medium heat and sauté the shallot for about a minute until it softens. Add the vermouth and reduce by half. Add the fish stock, the saffron liquid and some seasoning, bring to a boil and then remove from the heat.

Meanwhile, heat a grill pan over medium heat for 5 minutes. Cutting through the skin, slice the salmon fillet across into ½-inch strips. Brush the strips with oil on both sides, season on one side only and grill each side for 30–60 seconds (if you are using a non-stick grill pan you can omit the oil). You will probably need to cook the salmon strips in batches, reserving them on a plate once they are cooked.

At the same time, heat a tablespoon of oil in a large pan over high heat, add the baby spinach and sauté until it wilts. To serve, gently reheat the broth. Divide the spinach between four hot soup bowls, deep or shallow, ladle the broth over the spinach and arrange a few salmon strips in the center. Serve with small bowls of egg-fried rice on the side if desired (see below) and accompany with lemon or lime wedges.

On the side

Egg-fried rice

7 ounces basmati rice
sea salt, black pepper
2 medium eggs
1 tablespoon sesame oil

1 tablespoon peanut oil
4 scallions, trimmed and finely sliced
light soy sauce (optional), to serve

Rinse the rice in a sieve under cold water and place in a small saucepan with $1^1/3$ cups water and a teaspoon of salt. Bring to a boil and simmer over low heat for 8 minutes, and then remove from the heat, cover with a lid and leave to stand for 20 minutes.

Fluff up the rice using a fork, and whisk the eggs with the sesame oil and some seasoning in a bowl. Heat the peanut oil in a large pan over medium heat, add the eggs and then immediately add the rice and stir briskly to coat it. Cook for 2–3 minutes, turning it occasionally, and then remove from the heat and stir in the scallions. Season with a little soy sauce, if desired.

Thai hot and sour soup

A hot and sour Thai soup must be the culinary equivalent of reaching a mountain summit and taking a deep breath of crystal clean air. Its clarity is piercing, all those little spikes of flavor, and yet it's incredibly light compared to other fish stews – you could finish off a large bowl and still feel as though you could run around the block.

Serves 4

2 cups chicken stock
1 stalk of lemongrass, trimmed and thickly sliced
1 teaspoon finely chopped fresh ginger
3 lime leaves
1 small Thai red chile, finely sliced
18 ounces cleaned mussels (see page 78)
1 tablespoon peanut oil
2 small heads of bok choy, stems trimmed and leaves separated
12 raw shrimp, shelled*
2 tablespoons fish sauce
2 tablespoons lime juice
2 scallions, trimmed and finely sliced
1 heaping tablespoon chopped cilantro

Place the stock, lemongrass, ginger, lime leaves and chile in a medium saucepan. Bring to a boil, and then cover and simmer over low heat for 20 minutes.

Place the mussels in a saucepan, cover and steam open over high heat for 4–5 minutes. As soon as they are cool enough to handle, reserve about a third of them and shell the remainder. Place these together in a bowl and pour in the juices, discarding the last gritty bit.

Heat the oil in a large pan over medium heat, add the bok choy and sauté for a couple of minutes until the leaves turn dark green and wilt.

Strain the broth, return it to the pan and bring back to a boil. Add the bok choy and the shrimp, bring back to a boil and simmer for 1 minute. Stir in the fish sauce and lime juice. Add the mussels, along with their liquid, and heat through. Serve in warm soup bowls, scattered with the scallions and cilantro.

* If your shrimp arrive shell-on, carefully peel off their shells and add them to the soup base at the beginning, along with the other aromatics.

Portuguese fish stew

A north wind blows through this soup, with cabbage and potato there are characteristics of a comforting hash here. Its selling points are its gutsy rusticity, its ease of preparation and its affordability – compared to the expense so many fish soups can run up. It's great for all those little-known white fish fillets that greet us on the slab in the name of sustainability, which can be a deterrent when they don't come with a reference. Here you are unlikely to go wrong, so it's a good place to try them out. Dish it up with hearty slabs of grilled coarse-textured bread, splashed with olive oil.

Serves 6

3 ripe plum tomatoes

7 ounces Savoy cabbage, outer leaves removed

2 tablespoons extra virgin olive oil

7 ounces chorizo sausage (cooked or uncooked), skinned, thickly sliced and diced

2 pounds new potatoes, peeled and cut into ½-inch dice

½ cup white wine

6 cups fish stock

sea salt, black pepper

2 pounds mixed white fish fillets, skinned and cut into 1-inch pieces

extra virgin olive oil* and coarsely chopped cilantro, to serve

Bring a small pot of water to a boil, cut out the central core from each tomato, plunge them into the boiling water for about 20 seconds, and then into cold water. Skin and coarsely chop them. Slice the cabbage leaves into fine strands, discarding the tough central veins.

Heat the olive oil in a large saucepan over medium heat, add the chorizo and cook for a few minutes, stirring frequently, until lightly browned. Pour off the fat (leave this to harden before throwing away), and then add the potatoes. Give them a stir, and then add the wine and cook to reduce by half. Add the chopped tomatoes and fish stock and bring to a boil. Skim off any surface foam, and then simmer over low heat for 15 minutes. Coarsely mash the potato using a potato masher and season to taste with salt – the chorizo will have done most of the work here.

To serve, add the cabbage, bring back to a boil and simmer for 5 minutes. Season the fish with salt and pepper, add it to the soup and poach for 5 minutes. Serve in warm bowls with some olive oil poured over the top and a scattering of chopped fresh cilantro.

*A good case here for using your finest quality oil.

The Butcher

"Parsimony" is written in bold letters on the wall at the butcher. Soups have historically been a way of stretching meager rations and some of the finest traditions are born out of the act of being frugal, the idea of making a little go a long way. A few bits of bacon, a couple of spicy sausages, or chicken wings and drumsticks, will release their character into a broth, leaving a lingering sense of goodness. With the addition of lentils and beans, vegetables and herbs, more expensive cuts can also be stretched to double their value. A modest piece of lamb or pork can easily be turned into a soup to feed a crowd or into one that feeds just a few, but for a number of days. And it's not just the dog who benefits from befriending the butcher, most will happily wrap up unwanted bones for their regular customers for the purposes of making stock.

Harira

Harira is the most famous soup to come out of Morocco. Traditionally served during Ramadan, the ninth month of the Muslim calendar, it breaks the day's fast at sunset. It is easy to imagine just how good and nourishing it must seem, and why the Moroccans hold it so dear, with its gentle spices and the hearty comfort of lentils in a lamb broth.

Harira has a habit of seeming more complicated than it needs to be, inevitable perhaps when there is a long list of ingredients. Here I have pared it down and there's no sautéeing involved – just a couple of hours of gentle simmering. Neck fillet is especially good for this, but otherwise shoulder will do. You could add a handful or two of fine soup noodles a few minutes before the end of cooking.

Serves 6

2½ pounds loin of lamb, cut into
  thick medallions
2 medium onions, peeled and chopped
1 head of garlic, cloves peeled
a small bunch of thyme (about 10 sprigs), tied
sea salt
4 ripe tomatoes
10 ounces yellow split peas, rinsed
4 celery stalks, trimmed and finely sliced

¼ teaspoon crushed red pepper flakes
1 teaspoon turmeric
1 teaspoon ground ginger
½ teaspoon ground cinnamon
pinch of saffron (about 20 threads)
1 heaping teaspoon flour
juice of ½ lemon
3 tablespoons each finely chopped cilantro
  and flat-leaf parsley

Place the lamb in a large cast-iron dutch oven or other heavy-bottomed pot with the onion, garlic cloves, thyme, salt and 2 quarts of water. Bring to a boil, skim off the foam that rises to the surface, and then cover and cook over low heat for 30 minutes. Meanwhile, bring a small pot of water to a boil. Core the stems of the tomatoes by cutting out a cone from the top of each. Plunge the tomatoes into the boiling water for about 20 seconds and then into a bowl of cold water. Skin and coarsely chop.

Remove the lid from the dutch oven and add the split peas, celery, red pepper flakes, spices and tomatoes. Bring back to a boil, stirring, and then cover and simmer for another hour. Meanwhile, whisk the flour with the lemon juice in a small bowl.

To serve, stir the lemon juice mixture into the soup, bring back to a boil and simmer for another few minutes to cook the flour. Discard the thyme, stir in the chopped herbs and taste for seasoning. Ladle into warm bowls.

Bigos

This Polish hunters' stew would be even wilder at heart made with a jointed rabbit in lieu of chicken, using venison is also not unusual – although it would require longer cooking. *Bigos* varies hugely from one family and region to another, especially in the inclusion of meats. Poland's national dish, it is traditionally served on the second day of Christmas – although it is common for it to be stretched over the course of a week, periodically adding ingredients to the pot before it empties in the fashion of a medieval perpetual stew. This dish calls for one of those dark heavy rye breads to mop up the broth.

Serves 4–6

1 x 16-ounce jar of sauerkraut
¼ white cabbage, core discarded, finely shredded
sea salt, black pepper
1 tablespoon vegetable oil
2 medium onions, peeled, halved and sliced
4 ounces ready-to-eat, pitted prunes, halved

1 garlic clove, peeled and smashed
8 free-range chicken thighs
6 ounces Polish kielbasa *(or cooking chorizo sausage), skinned and thinly sliced*
2½ cups chicken stock
½ cup white wine

Drain the sauerkraut into a colander and rinse it under cold running water. Place in a medium saucepan and cover with water. Bring to a boil, and then drain again into the colander. Return it to the pan, cover with clean water and bring to a boil again, this time simmering it over low heat for 30 minutes. Prepare the white cabbage in exactly the same way, salting the second lot of water and cooking it for 15 minutes.

While the cabbage is cooking, heat the vegetable oil in a large pan over low heat and cook the onions for 20–25 minutes, stirring frequently, until golden and softened. Once the sauerkraut and cabbage are cooked, drain them in a colander and combine them in a bowl with the sautéed onions. Add the prunes and garlic clove, season with salt and pepper and combine well.

Preheat the oven to 350°F. Preheat the pan you used to cook the onions, season the chicken thighs and brown them on both sides, draining the fat as necessary. You will probably need to do this in two batches.

Arrange half the cabbage mixture in the base of a large heavy-bottomed pot. Place the chicken on top, scatter the sliced sausage over the chicken and top with the remaining cabbage. Season the chicken stock and pour it over the cabbage, along with the white wine. Cover with a lid and cook in the oven for 1½ hours, basting and pressing the cabbage down halfway through. Serve in warm, shallow bowls or on plates.

This takes inspiration from an Iranian or Persian lamb koresh, a stew that often contains rhubarb. Most soups benefit from a little acidity, something we often accomplish by adding a glass of wine, a tomato or two or a little lemon juice at the end. Here the rhubarb takes on that role.

Persian rhubarb soup with herbs

Serves 6

5–6 tablespoons extra virgin olive oil
2 large onions, peeled, halved and thinly sliced
1½ pounds loin of lamb, cut into 1-inch dice
leaves and fine stalks from 2 large bunches
   of parsley (about 3 ounces), coarsely chopped,
   plus extra to serve

2 ounces mint leaves, coarsely chopped
6 cups chicken stock
sea salt, black pepper
3½ ounces risotto rice, e.g. carnaroli
10½ ounces rhubarb (trimmed weight),
   cut into ½-inch lengths

Heat a couple of tablespoons of oil in a large heavy-bottomed pot or saucepan over medium heat, and cook the onion for 10–15 minutes until golden, stirring frequently. Transfer to a bowl, add another tablespoon of oil to the pan and color the meat – you will need to do this in batches. Reserve with the onions once it is done. Add another tablespoon of oil to the pan, put in the herbs and cook until they wilt. Return the lamb and onions to the pan, add the chicken stock and season with salt and pepper. Bring to a boil, and then cover and simmer for 40 minutes. You can prepare the soup to this point in advance.

Add the rice and simmer, covered, for another 15 minutes. Finally add the rhubarb and cook for 5 minutes. Serve with fresh parsley scattered over the top.

Lentil, lamb and frisee broth

Frisee cooks up every bit as well as its cousin Belgian endive, even though it is a little less usual, and its lacey fronds provide a delicate compliment to the lentils.

Serves 6

sea salt, black pepper
1½ pounds lamb chops
2 tablespoons vegetable or peanut oil
2 medium red onions, peeled, quartered
   and thinly sliced
6 ounces French green lentils, rinsed

1 sprig of rosemary, wrapped in a piece of muslin
1 cup white wine
6 cups lamb or chicken stock
½ head of frisee (mid and pale green parts),
   cut into roughly 1-inch fronds
coarsely chopped flat-leaf parsley, to serve

Preheat the oven to 300°F. Preheat a large pan over medium-high heat, season the lamb chops and brown them well on both sides – you will need to do this in batches, removing any excess fat as you go. Heat the oil in a large pot over medium heat, add the onion and cook for 10–15 minutes until softened and golden, stirring occasionally. Add the lamb chops, lentils, rosemary, wine, stock and some seasoning. Bring to a boil, skim off any foam from the surface, and then cover and cook in the oven for 1½ hours until the meat is meltingly tender.

Discard the rosemary and transfer the chops from the soup to a clean plate. Using two forks, flake the meat off the bones and then stir it back into the soup. You can prepare the soup to this point in advance.

To serve, reheat the soup and stir in the frisee. Ladle into warm bowls and sprinkle with parsley.

Pork and cauliflower stew with sherry and paprika

Here the cauliflower is the star ingredient, highlighted by the chorizo, sherry and chickpeas that lend a little Spanish charm to the dish and bring out the best in it. Romanesco cauliflower, with its beautifully-sculpted and colored spiral elements, might also find a home here in lieu of the standard ivory florets.

Serves 6

6–8 tablespoons extra virgin olive oil
4 medium onions, peeled, halved and sliced
3½ ounces chorizo, diced
½ teaspoon paprika
a pinch of saffron (about 20 threads)
sea salt, black pepper
1½ pounds pork loin, trimmed of fat and cut into ½-inch slices

½ cup medium sherry
12 ounces small cauliflower florets
12 ounces small broccoli florets
1 x 14-ounce can chickpeas, drained and rinsed
juice of ½ lemon
coarsely chopped flat-leaf parsley, to serve

Heat 3 tablespoons of oil in a large cast-iron pot over medium-low heat. Add the onions and cook for 15–25 minutes until syrupy and golden, stirring occasionally and adding the chorizo, paprika and saffron about 5 minutes before the end. Transfer everything to a bowl and keep to one side while you brown the pork. Turn up the heat and add another couple tablespoons of oil to the pan. You will need to brown the pork in two batches to avoid overcrowding the pan. Season the pork and sear on all sides, transferring it to the bowl with the onions as you go, and adding more oil to the pan as necessary.

Return the pork to the pan, along with the onion and chorizo mixture. Add the sherry, 1⅓ cups water and some seasoning. Bring to a boil, and then cover and cook over low heat for 1 hour.

Meanwhile, bring a large pan of salted water to a boil and blanch the cauliflower and broccoli florets for 2 minutes. Drain into a colander.

To serve, heat a tablespoon of oil in a large pan over medium-high heat and cook the cauliflower and broccoli until browned, seasoning well. You will need to do this in batches. Skim any excess fat off the stew, stir in the chickpeas and vegetables, cover and cook for a couple of minutes until just tender. Stir in the lemon juice, taste for seasoning and serve sprinkled with parsley.

Beet bouillon with steak and horseradish sauce

Beets and steak have a natural attraction for each other. The roots dye the broth a rich Renaissance hue, so this is on the dramatic side with its lily-white horseradish cream. Alternately, a teaspoon of grainy mustard is also delicious stirred into the crème fraîche if this fresh horseradish is hard to come by.

Serves 4

*2 tablespoons peanut oil, plus extra
    for brushing*
*1 medium red onion, peeled, halved and
    thinly sliced*
*2 small uncooked beets, trimmed, peeled
    and finely sliced*
½ cup red wine

2 cups beef stock
sea salt, black pepper
1 x 7-ounce sirloin steak, ½-inch thick
3½ ounces crème fraîche
2 teaspoons finely grated fresh horseradish
3½ ounces sugarsnap peas, topped and tailed

Heat a tablespoon of oil in a medium saucepan over medium heat, add the onion and sauté for a few minutes until softened. Add the beets and cook gently for a couple of minutes, turning it now and again. Pour in the wine and reduce by half. Add the beef stock and some seasoning, bring to a boil, and then cover and simmer over low heat for 20 minutes.

About 5 minutes into simmering the soup, heat a grill pan over medium heat for 5 minutes. Also bring a small pan of water to a boil. Brush the steak on both sides with oil and season it. Sear for about 2 minutes on each side to leave it medium-rare, and then transfer to a cutting board and leave to rest for 5 minutes.

Gently blend the crème fraîche and horseradish in a small bowl with a pinch of salt – don't stir too vigorously or the mixture will thicken and curdle. Blanch the sugarsnap pears in the boiling water for 1 minute, and then drain into a sieve. Cut the fat off the steak and slice it across into long strips.

Divide the beet soup between four warm, deep bowls. Place a few strips of steak to one side of each bowl and a pile of sugarsnap peas on the other. Dollop a spoonful of the horseradish sauce in the middle and serve immediately.

The Butcher

Spinach and beef stew with olives and pickled lemon

The spinach provides this soup with its wonderful inky-green color, while olives and pickled lemons keep the flavor bright. The best part is the rich juice so consider your pairings, my mind wanders to a crisp green, lightly dressed salad.

Serves 6

3–4 tablespoons extra virgin olive oil

1½ pounds diced beef cubes for stew (chunks roughly 1–1½ inches thick)

sea salt, black pepper

2 medium onions, peeled, halved and thinly sliced

3 garlic cloves, peeled and crushed to a paste

1 teaspoon ground cumin

¼ teaspoon ground allspice

a pinch of dried red pepper flakes

1½ pounds baby spinach leaves

6 ounces pitted green olives

a squeeze of fresh lemon juice

To serve

3 pickled lemons, finely sliced and seeds removed

a couple of handfuls of cilantro leaves

You will need to brown the meat in batches. Heat a couple of tablespoons of oil in a large cast-iron pot over high heat. Add the meat, season and sear to brown it all on all sides. Transfer to a clean plate while you brown the rest; keep to the side. Turn the heat down to medium, add the onion and cook for 5–7 minutes until browned, stirring occasionally. Stir in the garlic and spices, and then add the meat back to the pan. Add 1¼ cups water and some salt and bring to a boil. Cover and cook over low heat for 2 hours until the meat is tender.

Towards the end of this time, cook the spinach – you will need to do this in 3–4 batches. Heat a tablespoon of oil in a large pan over high heat, add a pile of spinach and cook it until it wilts, stirring. Transfer to a bowl and repeat with the remainder.

Stir the spinach and olives into the stew base and heat through, and then season with a squeeze of lemon juice. Combine the sliced pickled lemon and cilantro in a bowl and serve as a little relish on top of the stew.

Chicken mulligatawny

I took this soup on after my eldest son started to work his way through endless containers of a supermarket version. Even better than lentil soup, it contains shreds of chicken and that classic trio of ginger, garlic and chile, with lots of toppings to add at the end.

Serves 6

1 tablespoon peanut or vegetable oil
sea salt, black pepper
4 free-range chicken thighs
4 free-range chicken drumsticks
1–2 medium-hot red chiles, deseeded and
  finely sliced
2 tablespoons finely chopped fresh ginger
6 garlic cloves, peeled and finely sliced
6 shallots, peeled, halved and finely sliced
1 teaspoon turmeric

½ teaspoon ground cumin
½ teaspoon ground coriander
12 ounces yellow split peas, rinsed
5 cups chicken stock
1 x 14-ounce can of coconut milk
3–4 tablespoons fresh lemon juice
To serve
coarsely chopped cilantro, finely sliced scallions,
  finely sliced red chiles and coarsely
  chopped roasted peanuts

Heat the oil in a large saucepan over medium-high heat. Season the chicken and brown them on all sides, and then transfer them to a bowl. Turn the heat down, add the chile, ginger, garlic and shallot and cook briefly until softened and aromatic, stirring occasionally. Stir in the spices and the split peas and return the chicken to the pan. Add the stock and season with salt. Bring to a boil, and then cover and simmer for 45 minutes until the split peas are tender and the chicken is separating from the bone. Give the soup a stir towards the end to make sure the split peas aren't sticking.

Transfer the chicken pieces to a board or plate and shred the meat, discarding the skin and bones. Return the chicken to the soup, add the coconut milk and bring back to a boil. Season to taste with lemon juice and more salt, if necessary. Serve in warmed bowls sprinkled with the cilantro, scallions, chile and peanuts.

Lamb and butternut stew with pine nuts

Serves 6

5–6 tablespoons extra virgin olive oil

1½ pounds diced leg of lamb (chunks roughly 1 inch)

sea salt, black pepper

3 medium onions, peeled, halved and sliced

10 garlic cloves, peeled and thinly sliced

½ teaspoon ground allspice

½ teaspoon ground cinnamon

1 x 14-ounce can of chopped tomatoes

1 x 2-pound butternut squash

1 ounce pine nuts

1 ounce coarsely chopped flat-leaf parsley

1 ounce coarsely chopped cilantro

juice of ½ lemon

You will need to brown the lamb in batches. Heat a couple of tablespoons of oil in a large cast-iron pot over high heat, add half the lamb, season and sear to brown all over. Transfer this to a bowl while you brown the rest of the meat, adding a little more oil to the pan, if necessary. Keeping the meat to the side, turn the heat down to medium and cook the onions for 8–10 minutes until golden, stirring occasionally. Add the garlic towards the end and cook gently for a minute or so. Stir in the spices, and then add the tomatoes. Return the lamb to the pan, pour in 1¹/₃ cups water and season with salt and pepper. Bring to a boil, and then cover and cook over low heat for 1¼ hours or until the lamb is tender.

Meanwhile, cut the skin off the squash and chop it in half to separate the bulb from the trunk. Quarter the bulb, remove the seeds and slice into wedges; halve the trunk lengthways and cut into slices ¹/₃-inch thick.

When the stew is closed to finished, you can start cooking the squash – you will need to do this in batches. Heat a couple of tablespoons of oil in a large pan over high heat, add half the squash, season and brown it on both sides. Transfer to a clean plate while you brown the rest, again removing it at the end. Toast the pine nuts in the same pan, stirring constantly until golden. Reserve on a separate plate.

Once the lamb is cooked, stir the squash into the stew. Cover and cook for about 10 minutes until the squash is tender. To serve, stir in the herbs and lemon juice, taste for seasoning and sprinkle with the pine nuts.

This spicy Middle Eastern stew is another of those half and half dishes
— there is as much butternut squash as there is meat.
The result is too soupy to merit ladling over rice, some lovely
flatbread would be more the perfect partner.

Pot au feu

I love this take on the classic French assembly for its clear broth and the way the vegetables retain their color and shape. It is a simplified line-up, and a lighter one than the norm. The French would drink the soup and then eat the meat and vegetables separately, either hot with some gherkins and mustard, or cold with a vinaigrette, at which point either warm or cold new potatoes could come into play. The basil purée is optional, another thought is horseradish sauce* and chopped fresh parsley.

Serves 4

1 tablespoon peanut oil
2 pounds rump roast, trimmed of fat, cut into
*   2-inch chunks*
7 ounces bacon, cut into a 1-inch dice
sea salt, black pepper
4 leeks, trimmed and cut into ½-inch chunks
4 medium carrots, trimmed, peeled and sliced
*   on the diagonal ½-inch thick*

1 celery heart, trimmed and cut into ½-inch
*   pieces*
2 bay leaves
5 sprigs of thyme
Basil purée
1 garlic clove, peeled and chopped
2 ounces basil leaves
6 tablespoons extra virgin olive oil

You will need to brown the meat in batches to avoid overcrowding the pan. Heat the peanut oil in a large dutch oven over medium heat, add half the beef and bacon and sear on all sides. Transfer to a clean plate while you cook the rest. Return all the seared meat to the pan, add 7½ cups water, 1½ teaspoons of salt and some black pepper. Slowly bring to a simmer, skimming off the grayish foam as it rises to the surface. Add all the remaining ingredients for the stew, bring back to a simmer, and then cover and cook over low heat for 2 hours.

To make the basil purée, blend the garlic, basil, olive oil and some seasoning in a food processor and reduce to a smooth purée.

To serve, remove the bay leaf and thyme from the stew and ladle into bowls, placing a spoonful of the basil purée in the center of each.

* For the simplest and best horseradish sauce, gently blend 1 x 7-ounce container of crème fraîche with
2–3 tablespoons finely grated horseradish and season with salt.

Fava bean and chicken stew with pomegranate

This is a stew prepared in reverse. First you poach your chicken, which creates the base of the stock, and then you lightly cook the vegetables in the stock before throwing in lots of herbs at the end.

Serves 6

Chicken base
3–4 tablespoons extra virgin olive oil
sea salt, black pepper
6 pieces of free-range chicken, for example
    thighs and drumsticks
1 onion, peeled and halved
1 bay leaf
1 cinnamon stick, about 2 inches in length
Stew
3 medium onions, peeled and chopped
2 celery stalks, trimmed and sliced
4 garlic cloves, peeled and finely chopped

14 ounces leeks (trimmed weight), sliced
½ teaspoon ground ginger
¼ teaspoon allspice
18 ounces cooked baby fava beans*
14 ounces small turnips, peeled and cut into
    thin wedges or diced
several large handfuls of coarsely chopped
    cilantro
several large handfuls of coarsely chopped dill
juice of ½–1 lemon
seeds of 1 pomegranate, to serve

Heat a couple of tablespoons of oil in a large dutch oven over high heat. Season the chicken pieces and add to the pan, browning them on all sides. Spoon off the excess fat, add 2 cups water, the halved onion, bay leaf and cinnamon stick. Don't worry if the chicken isn't completely covered. Bring to a boil, and then cover and cook over low heat for 1 hour until the chicken is tender. Carefully lift out the chicken pieces and strain the liquid into a large bowl.

Heat 2 tablespoons of oil in the cleaned out dutch oven over medium heat. Add the chopped onion and celery and cook for several minutes until softened, stirring occasionally. Put in the garlic and leeks and cook for a couple of minutes. Stir in the ginger and allspice, add the fava beans and turnips, and pour in the chicken poaching liquid. Season with salt and pepper. Bring to a boil, and then cover and simmer for 15 minutes.

Meanwhile, shred the chicken meat, discarding the skin and bones. To serve, add the chicken to the soup and heat through. Stir in the herbs and lemon juice, taste for seasoning and scatter the pomegranate seeds over the top.

I normally use frozen baby fava beans, and cook them according to the instructions on the package. If using fresh ones, simmer for about 7 minutes until tender.

Chicken and mushroom noodle soup

This is a noodle dish with an Eastern sensibility, a very light broth with noodles, chicken and mushrooms. There is nothing worse than an tasteless broth, so this calls for a really good homemade chicken stock, and I tend to reduce it by about a third to enrich its flavor.

Serves 4

2 skinless free-range chicken breasts
1 tablespoon peanut oil, plus extra
*   for brushing*
sea salt, black pepper
2 cups good homemade chicken stock
1 tablespoon dry sherry
2 tablespoons light soy sauce
2 ounces fine rice noodles

2 shallots, peeled and finely chopped
6 ounces mixed wild mushrooms, picked over and
*   sliced if necessary*
To serve
1 medium-hot red chile, deseeded, finely sliced
3 scallions, trimmed and sliced on the
*   diagonal*
coarsely chopped cilantro

Preheat a grill pan over medium heat for 5 minutes, brush the chicken breasts on both sides with oil and season them. Grill for 3–4 minutes on each side until the outside is charred with golden stripes, and the breast feels firm when pressed with your finger. Transfer to a cutting board and leave to rest for 5 minutes.

Bring the chicken stock to a boil in a small saucepan, and then remove from the heat and stir in the sherry and soy sauce. Place the noodles in a bowl, cover with boiling water and stir to separate them. Leave to soak for 3 minutes or as directed on the package. Heat a tablespoon of oil in a large pan over medium heat, add the shallots and sauté for about a minute until they soften. Add the mushrooms and sauté for a few minutes to soften them, seasoning halfway through.

To serve, drain the noodles into a colander and divide between four warm, deep soup bowls. Spoon the mushrooms to one side and ladle in the soup liquid. Slice the chicken breasts and arrange a few slices in the center of each bowl of soup. Sprinkle with the chile, scallion and cilantro.

Poule au pot

Despite the way my elderly French neighbor's eyes glaze over as he describes his mother's *poule au pot*, I have yet to have any success cooking this dish with the real bird, which is older than a roasting chicken. The resulting stock may indeed be delicious, and perhaps that is what such birds are best reserved for, but the flesh itself, which is traditionally enjoyed with a simple cream sauce, tends to be dry and unpleasantly tough, regardless of how long you cook it for.

Here the method employs a roasting chicken that is effectively pot-roasted – you can use bouillon cubes for the initial stock. The chicken is carved up and served alongside the vegetables, while the resulting liquid, of which there will be a nice amount left over, can be added to a new stockpot using the carcass. So it's a dish with two lives, or at least a particularly fine stock at the very end. It's simple and nurturing, the sort of soup my family insists I take to them in bed when they are laid up with any sort of bug, with some very thin toast. Whatever bread you do serve, a good salty butter will be delicious slathered over it.

Serves 4–6

1 x 3½-pound free-range chicken
peanut oil, for brushing
sea salt, black pepper
4 narrow carrots, trimmed and peeled,
    halved if long
2 leeks, trimmed and thickly sliced
1 celery heart, trimmed and thickly sliced
    on the diagonal

4 garlic cloves, peeled
½ cup white wine
6 cups chicken stock
1 bay leaf
a few sprigs of thyme
coarsely chopped flat-leaf parsley, to serve

Heat a large pan over medium-high heat. Lightly coat the chicken all over with oil and season with salt and pepper. Sear the chicken on all sides to brown it, and then place it in a large heavy-bottomed pot. Put in all the remaining ingredients, except for the parsley, so that the liquid covers the chicken by about two-thirds. Bring to a boil, and then cover and cook over low heat for 55 minutes.

Lift out the bird and transfer to a warm plate to rest for 15–20 minutes, draining the juices inside back into the pot. Bring the heat up to high and boil the liquid to concentrate its flavor until it is reduced by about a quarter. Skim off any matter as it rises to the surface and take out the herbs. Carve the chicken and serve with the vegetables and a little soup, sprinkled with parsley. Use the leftover liquid and the carcass to start a second stock.

Spicy coconut chicken soup

This soup has many ingredients in common with the Chicken mulligatawny (see page 112), but it is lighter – more of a coconut broth with a few veggies and shreds of chicken.

Serves 4

2 garlic cloves, peeled
1 teaspoon finely chopped medium-hot red chile
1-inch piece of fresh ginger, peeled and
    coarsely chopped
2 tablespoons peanut oil
3 shallots, peeled and finely sliced
2 medium carrots, trimmed, peeled and
    finely sliced

1 x 14-ounce can of coconut milk
2 cups chicken stock
2 skinless free-range chicken breasts
2 tablespoons fish sauce
a couple of squeezes of lemon or lime juice
½ teaspoon sugar
2 scallions, trimmed and finely sliced
coarsely chopped cilantro, to serve

Place the garlic, chile and ginger in a small blender, such as a coffee grinder, and reduce to a paste. Heat the oil in a medium saucepan over medium heat, add the paste and cook it momentarily to release all the flavors. Quickly put in the shallots and carrots and cook for a couple of minutes, stirring frequently, until nice and glossy. Pour in the coconut milk and chicken stock, bring to a boil and simmer over low heat for 10 minutes.

Meanwhile, prepare the chicken. Cut out and discard the white tendon underneath each chicken breast, and then cut into thin strips. Add the chicken to the soup and simmer for 2 minutes. Stir in the fish sauce, the lemon or lime juice and the sugar. Ladle the soup into small deep bowls, piling the chicken and vegetables in the center. Sprinkle with some scallion and cilantro to serve.

Chicken noodle soup

This is the classic chicken noodle soup, almost worth developing a cold for the treat of sipping it while propped up in bed. It's the great restorative. If vermicelli soup noodles are hard to come by, gently crush vermicelli nests between your fingers to break them up. Otherwise there are all kinds of tiny pastas that will provide the right degree of comfort.

Serves 4

2 tablespoons unsalted butter
3 leeks, trimmed and thinly sliced
½ cup white wine
5 cups chicken stock
sea salt, black pepper

3 ounces short vermicelli or other soup noodles
2 skinless free-range chicken breasts
1 tablespoon extra virgin olive oil
3 tablespoons finely chopped parsley
freshly grated Parmesan, to serve

Melt the butter in a medium saucepan over medium-low heat and cook the leeks for 5–7 minutes until they begin to soften, stirring occasionally. Add the wine, turn the heat up and cook to reduce it by half. Add the chicken stock, season and bring to a boil. Simmer over low heat for 10 minutes, stirring in the vermicelli soup noodles halfway through – if you are using a different type of pasta then adjust the cooking time accordingly, bearing in mind they should be lovely and soft rather than al dente.

While the soup base is cooking, prepare the chicken. Cut out the tendon from underneath each of the breasts and slice them into two thin escalopes. Now slice across into thin strips. Heat the olive oil in a large pan over medium-high heat, add the chicken and cook for a minute or two to seal it, stirring frequently. Turn the heat up and cook for a few minutes longer until starting to turn golden, seasoning towards the end of cooking.

To serve, stir the parsley and chicken into the soup, adjust the seasoning and ladle into warm bowls. Accompany with grated Parmesan.

The Grocer

Any shop that makes a virtue out of selling lentils, dried beans, rice and pasta is
to be cherished. I can lose myself for hours among the shelves of an old-fashioned
grocer, examining all of the different products, strange cans and jars,
with the same wonder I had while peering into a doll's house as a child.
Grocers are for exploring, they offer insight into the culture at hand, be it
Greek, Chinese, Italian or Middle Eastern. They make for delightful
shopping, providing the ingredients for the most nurturing soups of all.
I have not tried to hide my love of lentil and other bean soups in what follows,
I could happily make and eat these every day.

Middle Eastern lentil soup
with pomegranate syrup

Serves 6

4 tablespoons extra virgin olive oil,
  plus extra to serve
4 medium carrots, trimmed, peeled and
  finely chopped
1 celery heart, trimmed and finely sliced
2 medium onions, peeled and finely chopped
6 garlic cloves, peeled and finely chopped
1 tablespoon coarsely crushed coriander seeds

¼ teaspoon crushed red pepper flakes
8 ounces red lentils
8 ounces yellow split peas
2 quarts chicken or vegetable stock, or water
sea salt
pomegranate syrup (or lemon juice), and
  coarsely chopped cilantro, to serve

Heat the olive oil in a large saucepan over medium-low heat. Add the carrot, celery, onion and garlic and cook for 15–20 minutes until soft and aromatic, stirring occasionally. Stir in the crushed coriander seeds and red pepper flakes. Rinse the lentils and split peas in a sieve under cold water, add them to the pan and cook for 4–5 minutes, stirring occasionally. Pour in the stock or water, bring to a boil and simmer over low heat for 1 hour – by which time the split peas should be nice and soft. Season to taste with salt.

Ladle the soup into warmed bowls. To serve, drizzle a little pomegranate syrup over each serving, then some olive oil and finally sprinkle with plenty of chopped cilantro.

Very Monterey soup

This one checks all the "hippie" boxes, none of which have changed since Scott McKenzie suggested you needed to wear flowers in your hair if you were going to San Francisco. A smooth red lentil soup, as good for weaning babies as for comforting older generations, most of whom hung up their sandals long ago.

Serves 6

4 tablespoons extra virgin olive oil
2 leeks, trimmed and sliced
4 medium carrots, trimmed, peeled and sliced
1 celery heart, trimmed and sliced
1 heaping tablespoon finely chopped
  fresh ginger
1 heaping teaspoon finely chopped medium-hot
  red chile

4 garlic cloves, peeled and finely chopped
18 ounces red lentils, rinsed
3 tablespoons cider vinegar
2 quarts chicken or vegetable stock
sea salt
Greek or sheep's milk yogurt and coarsely chopped
  flat-leaf parsley, to serve

Heat the olive oil in a large saucepan over medium heat, add the leeks, carrots, celery, ginger and chile and cook for about 10 minutes until softened and beginning to brown, then add the garlic and cook for a few minutes longer. Stir in the lentils, add the cider vinegar, pour in the stock and season with salt. Bring to a boil, skim off any surface foam and simmer for 30 minutes or until the lentils are tender. Purée in batches in a blender, and then taste for seasoning. Serve with a dollop of yogurt and lots of parsley.

Pomegranate syrup is lovely stuff, it hits the same notes as balsamic vinegar without the price tag. Here a succinct drizzle works its sweet and sour magic with some chopped cilantro, which is always a breath of fresh air.

Spicy red lentil soup with garlic raita

The garlic *raita*? Well that ensures that nothing is left to chance, though in truth you don't have to go through the trouble of roasting a head of garlic – the yogurt on its own will do. I frequently have a container of *tzatziki* in the fridge, a great low-fat snack standby, and that would work equally well here.

Serves 4

2 tablespoons unsalted butter
2 garlic cloves, peeled and finely chopped
1 heaping teaspoon finely chopped
    fresh ginger
12 ounces leeks (trimmed weight), sliced
9 ounces red lentils, rinsed
10 ounces ripe tomatoes, skinned (see page 134)
    and chopped
2 whole medium-hot red chiles

1 heaping teaspoon ground cumin
1 heaping teaspoon ground coriander
¼ teaspoon turmeric
1½ teaspoons sea salt
1 tablespoon lemon or lime juice
coarsely chopped cilantro, to serve

Raita
1 large head of garlic
5 tablespoons Greek yogurt

Start with the *raita*. preheat the oven to 400°F. Slice the top off the head of garlic, wrap it in foil and roast for 20–30 minutes, then allow it to cool.

While the garlic for the *raita* is roasting, make the soup. Melt the butter in a large saucepan, add the finely chopped fresh garlic, the ginger and the sliced leeks and cook over low heat for several minutes without allowing to brown. Add the lentils, tomatoes, chiles, spices, salt and 2 quarts water. Bring to a boil, skim off any surface foam and simmer for 30–40 minutes, stirring occasionally. Add the lemon or lime juice, discard the chiles and adjust the seasoning.

While the soup is cooking, finish making the *raita*. Squeeze the cooked inside of the roasted garlic into a bowl and mash it with the Greek yogurt and a little salt. Ladle the hot soup into warm bowls and serve with a dollop of *raita* and plenty of chopped cilantro sprinkled on top.

Lentils are at their best married with lots of aromatics, they're a great vehicle for carrying spices, garlic, chile, lemon and the like. They provide a base note within a soup, and their hearty texture contrasts really well with silky vegetables like tomatoes and leeks.

Nada's Syrian grain soup

This healthy and nourishing soup is derived from my friend Nada Saleh's book *Seductive Flavours of the Levant*, a tour of the home cooking of Lebanon, Syria and Turkey. I love the combination of lentils, rice and bulgur wheat – far from being over-carbed, each ingredient brings a different texture and flavor to the soup, and the method itself is unusual. All the interest is added at the end rather than at the beginning, a departure from how we tend to approach soups in the west.

Serves 4

9 ounces red lentils, rinsed
3 ounces short-grain rice, rinsed
3 ounces coarse bulgur wheat
sea salt

4 tablespoons extra virgin olive oil,
*   plus extra to serve*
2 medium onions, peeled, halved and finely sliced
1 teaspoon ground cumin
½ lemon

Combine the lentils, rice, bulgur wheat and 2 quarts water in a medium saucepan. Bring to a boil over high heat, skim any foam from the surface, and then reduce the heat to medium. Sprinkle in 2 teaspoons of salt, partially cover with a lid and simmer for 15 minutes or until the grains are tender.

Meanwhile, heat the oil in a large pan over medium heat until hot but not smoking. Add the onions and cook for about 15 minutes until golden brown, stirring occasionally.

Stir the fried onions and cumin into the soup, adjust the seasoning and serve in warm bowls with a little fresh-squeezed lemon juice and a drizzle of oil. Serve with crusty bread and a side dish of scallions, mint and olives, if desired (see below).

Syrian meze

On the side

8 scallions, trimmed
a handful of mint leaves
2 ounces green olives, pitted

crusty white bread, to serve 4
extra virgin olive oil

Arrange the scallions, mint and olives in piles on a plate, with the bread and oil plated separately. Allow everyone to help themselves, dipping the bread in the oil and eating it with the scallions, mint and olives.

Wintery spelt soup

I feel like this ancient grain's publicist, and one can't get enough of it, so if you are unfamiliar with it let me introduce you. It is thought to be a hybrid of emmer wheat and goat's grass, that is, it preceded modern wheat. Spelt has a loyal following among those who suffer wheat intolerance. It does contain gluten, but spelt has a different structure that many find easier to digest.

My own appreciation, however, lies in the eating. Spelt is positively suave, which isn't always a word I associate with grains, more Tom Ford than Gerard Dépardieu. It also has one up on farro, with which it is often confused, as it doesn't require soaking. Its rather close to barley too, but spelt is tender in under 20 minutes.

Here it is woven into a wintery bowl of goodness with bacon, cabbage, a hint of chile and lots of parsley. Try it in other soups with vegetables too like butternut squash and red onion, broccoli and fava beans – and it laps up olive oil, garlic, spices and other leafy herbs, such as cilantro and mint.

Serves 4

2 tablespoons extra virgin olive oil
6 ounces unsmoked pancetta or bacon, diced
3 garlic cloves, peeled and finely chopped
1 teaspoon finely sliced medium-hot red chile
2 ripe tomatoes, skinned (see page 134)
    and chopped
1 cup pearled spelt, rinsed

4½ cups chicken or vegetable stock
½ small Savoy cabbage (about 10 ounces), cut into
    wide strips with tough white parts discarded
6 tablespoons coarsely chopped flat-leaf parsley,
    plus extra to serve
sea salt
freshly grated Parmesan, to serve

Heat the olive oil in a large saucepan over medium heat, add the pancetta or bacon and cook for 5–8 minutes until lightly golden, stirring occasionally. Add the garlic and chile and cook for a minute until fragrant. Add the tomatoes and cook for a few minutes until mushy, then stir in the spelt. Add the stock, bring to a boil and simmer for 15 minutes, then stir in the cabbage and cook for 5 minutes more. Stir in the parsley and adjust the seasoning. Serve with extra parsley scattered over the top, accompanied by the Parmesan.

Puy lentil, spinach and bacon soup

Serves 6

7 ounces Puy lentils
18 ounces ripe tomatoes on the vine
1 tablespoon extra virgin olive oil, plus extra to serve
6 ounces bacon, diced
2 medium red onions, peeled and chopped
4 garlic cloves, peeled and finely chopped
½ cup white wine
14 ounces baby spinach
1¾ cups chicken or vegetable stock
sea salt, black pepper
6 tablespoons coarsely chopped flat-leaf parsley

Bring a large pan of water to a boil, add the lentils and simmer for 20–30 minutes or until tender, then drain them into a sieve. At the same time, bring a medium pan of water to a boil, cut out a cone from the top of each tomato, plunge into the boiling water for about 20 seconds, and then into cold water. Slip off the skins and coarsely chop the flesh.

Heat a tablespoon of olive oil in a large saucepan over medium heat, add the bacon and cook for 7–8 minutes until golden, stirring occasionally. Transfer to a bowl using a slotted spoon. Add the onion and cook for 10–15 minutes until softened and lightly golden, stirring frequently. Add the garlic and cook for a couple of minutes, and then return the bacon to the pan. Stir in the tomatoes and cook for 3–5 minutes until they collapse. Add the wine and simmer to reduce it by half.

Add the spinach, turn up the heat and cook until it wilts, stirring occasionally. Stir in the cooked lentils, add the stock and plenty of seasoning and bring to a boil, then stir in the parsley. The soup can be made in advance and gently reheated, although you will lose the vibrant green of the spinach. Serve with a few goat's cheese crostini, either on the side or floating in the soup, if you desired (see below).

On the side

Goat cheese crostini

A little button flavored with rosemary, juniper berries and chile. Try to find a good quality, local goat cheese for this tasty bite.

12 thin slices of baguette
7 ounces medium-mature goat cheese, thinly sliced
extra virgin olive oil, to drizzle

Preheat the broiler. Arrange the slices of baguette on a baking sheet, lay the goat cheese on top, drizzle with oil and broil until golden and crusty.

This is on the brothy side compared to soups based on red lentils or yellow split peas, both of which simmer down almost into a purée. Puy lentils hold their shape and provide a distinctive bite.

French green lentil soup with Roquefort

Shopping for green lentils can prove to be confusing. Le Puy lentils are both green and French, and yet we refer to the softer mealy green lentils as "French green lentils." They are really quite different, the latter are softer, while Le Puy lentils are small, composed little peas by comparison. This soup plays on the success of traditional split pea soup and it is the softer green lentils that are called for here.

Serves 4

1 tablespoon peanut oil

3½ ounces bacon, diced

2 medium onions, peeled, halved and sliced

2 garlic cloves, peeled and finely chopped

⅔ cup red wine

7 ounces French green lentils, rinsed

1 bay leaf

1 dried red chile, finely chopped

6 cups chicken stock

sea salt

Roquefort Cream

3 ounces Roquefort, crumbled

3 ounces crème fraîche

Tabasco

Heat the oil in a large saucepan over medium heat, add the bacon and the onion and cook for 12–15 minutes until lightly caramelized, adding the garlic just before the end. Add the red wine and cook down until syrupy. Add the lentils, the bay leaf, the chile and the chicken stock. Bring to a simmer and cook for 40 minutes. Season generously with salt.

While the soup is cooking, mash the Roquefort and crème fraîche together in a bowl and season with a dash of Tabasco. Serve the soup in warm bowls, with a spoon of the Roquefort cream in the middle.

Quick fasolada

This bean soup is one of the national treasures of the Greek table, and much quicker to prepare if you cheat with canned white beans and chopped tomatoes. It will be just as colorful as if you had slaved over it for hours, and there's little that a good olive oil won't sort out, drizzled over it at the end.

Serves 4

4 tablespoons extra virgin olive oil, plus extra to serve

1 medium onion, peeled and chopped

4 medium carrots, trimmed, peeled, halved lengthways and thinly sliced

1 celery heart, trimmed and thinly sliced

3 garlic cloves, peeled and finely chopped

2 x 14-ounce cans of cannellini or other white beans, drained and rinsed

1 x 14-ounce can of chopped tomatoes

1 quart vegetable or chicken stock

sea salt, black pepper

6 tablespoons coarsely chopped flat-leaf parsley

Heat 4 tablespoons oil in a large saucepan over medium-low heat and cook the onion, carrot and celery for about 20 minutes until transluscent and softened, adding the garlic just before the end. Add the drained beans and give them a stir, then the tomatoes, stock and some seasoning. Bring to a boil and simmer for 15 minutes. Stir in the parsley, adjust the seasoning and serve with plenty of good olive oil drizzled on top.

Two-lentil soup with caramelized onions and lemon

When I first ate this soup at a local café, it was a revelation. The soup itself was relatively dull, but it was smothered with slowly caramelized onions and served with a generous squeeze of lemon juice and some olive oil. It was fab. Point learned was that you don't have to weave all the interest into a soup as it simmers – by adding grace notes at the end you frequently get a livelier result than simply trying to doctor the broth with more of this or that. Here the onions take a little time, so if you don't have it there are faster options – for example, a sprinkling of chopped fresh parsley or cilantro, along with a good spritz of lemon juice and olive oil.

Serves 4–6

4 tablespoons extra virgin olive oil
4 medium carrots, trimmed, peeled and sliced
1 celery heart, trimmed and sliced
2 medium red onions, peeled and chopped
2-inch piece of fresh ginger, peeled and finely chopped
6 garlic cloves, peeled and finely chopped
8 ounces red lentils
8 ounces yellow split peas

2 quarts vegetable stock
sea salt, black pepper
To serve
2 tablespoons extra virgin olive oil, plus extra for drizzling
2 large onions (ideally white), peeled, halved and sliced as finely as possible
4 squeezes of lemon juice

Heat the olive oil for the soup in a large saucepan over medium-low heat, add the carrot, celery, red onion, ginger and garlic and cook, stirring occasionally, for about 20 minutes until soft and aromatic. Rinse the lentils and split peas in a sieve under the cold water, and then add them to the pan. Cook for 4–5 minutes, stirring occasionally. Add the vegetable stock, bring to a boil and simmer over low heat for 1 hour – by which time the split peas should be nice and mushy.

While the soup is cooking, heat 2 tablespoons olive oil in a large pan over very low heat. Add the finely sliced onions and cook for 40–50 minutes, stirring frequently, especially towards the end when they are more liable to catch and burn. By the end, they should be a deep even golden color. Transfer to a bowl.

Process the soup in batches in a blender with some salt and pepper – it should be very thick, the consistency of a thin purée. Ladle it into warmed soup bowls, squeeze a little lemon juice over each serving and drizzle with some olive oil. Finally distribute the caramelized onions over the top.

Plum tomato soup with green lentils

Many of my favorite lentil soups are the kind that carry you from lunch to supper without any pangs of hunger. But this soup is an exception. Here the French green lentils play only a small part, just a few in a tomato soup pepped up with chile, and lots of parsley stirred in at the end. Light enough to provide us with an excuse for a mid-afternoon snack, unless you take into account the marinated shrimp suggested as an accompaniment.

Serves 4

6 tablespoons extra virgin olive oil, plus extra to serve

2 medium onions, peeled and chopped

2 medium carrots, trimmed, peeled and thinly sliced

2 celery stalks, trimmed and thinly sliced

1 heaping teaspoon finely chopped medium-hot red chile

4 garlic cloves, peeled and finely chopped

3½ pounds ripe beefsteak or plum tomatoes

3½ ounces French green lentils, rinsed

a pinch of saffron (about 20 threads)

1 teaspoon sugar

sea salt

6 tablespoons coarsely chopped flat-leaf parsley

Heat 3 tablespoons olive oil in a large saucepan over medium heat and cook the onion, carrot, celery and chile for 10–15 minutes, stirring frequently, until lightly browned, adding the garlic halfway through.

At the same time, bring a medium pot of water to a boil, cut out a small cone from the top of each tomato to remove the core, and then plunge them into the boiling water for about 20 seconds (you may need to do this in batches). Immediately transfer them to a bowl of cold water, and then slip off the skins and coarsely chop the flesh.

Add the tomatoes, lentils, saffron, sugar and 1⅓ cups water to the vegetables and bring to a boil. Cover and cook over low heat for 35–40 minutes or until the lentils are tender. Season the soup with salt, and add half the parsley and 3 tablespoons of olive oil. Serve in warm bowls, drizzled with a little extra oil and sprinkled with the rest of the parsley. Serve with the shrimp brochettes if desired (see below).

On the side ## Shrimp brochettes

7 ounces shelled raw large shrimp (ideally tail-on)

1-inch piece of fresh ginger, peeled and coarsely grated

2 garlic cloves, peeled and crushed into a paste

2 tablespoons extra virgin olive oil

sea salt, black pepper

¼ lemon

Thread the shrimp onto four 6-inch skewers. Mix the ginger and garlic with the olive oil on a plate, or in a shallow container. Coat the shrimp with the marinade, and then cover and chill for a couple of hours (ideally overnight), but if you are in a rush you can grill them right away.

Preheat a grill pan, season the skewers and cook them for 1–2 minutes on the first side, and about 1 minute on the second. Squeeze a little fresh lemon juice over them to serve.

The Grocer

Scotch broth

Barley is the defining ingredient here, with its satisfyingly slippery and wholesome goodness, served in a broth sweetened by lamb and packed with nourishing, soft winter vegetables. You can dice the vegetables quite small for this – which would be ideal, but I don't want to put you under any pressure – you can also leave them that little bit larger and provide a fork with the spoon for mashing them into the broth as you go.

Serves 6

1 bay leaf

*18 ounces loin of lamb, halved lengthways and
    sliced ½-inch thick*

10 ounces turnips, trimmed, peeled and diced

10 ounces rutabaga, peeled and diced

*10 ounces new potatoes, scrubbed or peeled
    as necessary, and diced*

1 leek, trimmed and thinly sliced

1 celery heart, trimmed and thinly sliced

*2 medium carrots, trimmed, peeled, halved
    lengthways and sliced*

sea salt, black pepper

2 quarts chicken stock

3½ ounces pearled barley

*6 tablespoons coarsely chopped
    flat-leaf parsley, to serve*

Combine all the ingredients except for the parsley in a large heavy-bottomed pot. Bring to a boil and skim off any foam as it rises to the surface – you may need to do this a couple of times in the early stages of simmering. Cook over low heat for 1 hour. Stir in the parsley and season to taste. The soup can be made in advance and reheated, in which case scrape off the fat on the surface once it has cooled.

Ham and barley soup with mustard cream

A great post-Christmas favorite in our house, this turns all sorts of leftover goodies into a potful of comfort. If you cooked your own ham for Christmas, the stock can be put to good use here – although depending on how salty it is, you might need to dilute it with turkey or chicken stock.

Serves 6

4 tablespoons unsalted butter

1 celery heart, trimmed and sliced

*2 large carrots (about 9 ounces), trimmed,
    peeled and thinly sliced on the diagonal*

2 leeks, trimmed and thinly sliced

3 ounces pearled barley

2 quarts ham or chicken stock

*6 thin slices of ham, fat removed, cut into
    1 x 2-inch strips*

5½ ounces crème fraîche

1 tablespoon Dijon mustard

sea salt, black pepper

coarsely chopped flat-leaf parsley, to serve

Melt the butter in a large saucepan over medium heat, add the celery, carrot and leeks and cook for 5 minutes, stirring occasionally, until translucent but not browned. Stir in the pearled barley and cook for a minute or two, stirring. Add the stock, bring to a boil and simmer over low heat for 30 minutes or until the barley is tender, adding the ham just before the end. Meanwhile, blend the crème fraîche and mustard in a bowl. Season the soup with black pepper and salt, if necessary. Serve in warm bowls with the mustard cream spooned in the center, sprinkled with parsley.

Russian mushroom soup

There's enough Russian spirit here with the wild mushrooms, dill and sour cream to conjure up warmth on a cold winter's day. It can be turned into an even heartier bowlful with a pile of noodles and more wild mushrooms scattered over it, or eaten on the side (see below).

You could also boost the flavor further with the addition of some dried wild mushrooms. Cover 1 ounce dried mushrooms with 1 cup boiling stock (taken from the total amount) and leave to soak for 15 minutes. Add the drained mushrooms along with all of the cooked vegetables, and add the soaking liquid with the rest of the stock.

Serves 6

8 ounces wild or interesting cultivated mushrooms (shiitake, chanterelles, etc.)
2 tablespoons unsalted butter
14 ounces white mushrooms, sliced
1 medium onion, peeled and chopped
1 leek, trimmed and sliced

1 small fennel bulb, trimmed and chopped
½ cup white wine
6 cups chicken or vegetable stock
sea salt, black pepper
½ cup heavy cream

Pick over all the wild mushrooms, scrape or wipe them if they are dirty and slice them if necessary.

You will need to cook the vegetables in batches to avoid overcrowding the pan. Melt the butter in a large saucepan over medium heat and cook the mushrooms, onion, leek and fennel together until softened. If the mushrooms release any juices, reserve them along with the cooked vegetables.

Place all the cooked vegetables back into the saucepan, add the wine and cook to reduce it by half. Add the stock and some seasoning, bring to a boil and simmer for 15 minutes. Purée the soup in batches and return to the pan. If you want a really smooth soup, you could blend it again. Stir in the cream. The soup can be made to this point in advance.

Close to the time of serving, reheat the soup if necessary, ladle into warm bowls and serve with the Mushroom noodles (see below) if desired.

On the side ## Mushroom noodles

3½ ounces thin egg noodles
2 tablespoons unsalted butter
2 shallots, peeled and finely chopped
8 ounces wild mushrooms (prepared as above)

sea salt, black pepper
a squeeze of fresh lemon juice
½ cup sour cream
chopped dill

Bring a pot of salted water to a boil. Add the noodles, stir to separate them and cook until tender, leaving them al dente. Drain and reserve in a sieve. Melt the butter in a large pan over medium-high heat and cook the shallot for a minute or two. Add the mushrooms and toss until they soften, then season with salt, pepper and a squeeze of fresh lemon juice. Add the noodles to the pan and gently heat together, tasting for seasoning. Pile the mushroom noodles in the center of the soup, dollop with some sour cream and scatter with the dill.

Pistou

A great heatwave soup, for those rare days when it's so hot you plan to get everything including the cooking out of the way before mid-morning. Then you can settle down to a leisurely lunch of newly cooled *pistou* with a bottle of chilled rosé before retiring for a siesta.

Serves 4

1 quart vegetable stock or water

18 ounces mixed green summer vegetables, diced or sliced, e.g. zucchini, green beans, celery

2 ounces short vermicelli or other soup noodles (see page 124)

2 x 10-ounce cans of flageolet or lima beans, drained and rinsed

1½ ounces basil leaves

5 ounces freshly grated Parmesan

4 garlic cloves, peeled

¼ cup extra virgin olive oil, plus extra to serve

sea salt, black pepper

Bring the stock or water to a boil, add the vegetables and soup noodles and simmer for 10 minutes, adding the canned beans just before the end. Blend the basil, Parmesan, garlic and olive oil in a food processor and stir into the cooked soup, then season to taste. Serve with a little more oil drizzled over the top.

Quick chickpea and cabbage soup

I have had variable success at ridding dried chickpeas of their chalky heart – something that has everything to do with how fresh they are. Canned chickpeas guarantee tenderness.

Serves 4

5 tablespoons unsalted butter

2 medium onions, peeled and chopped

1 celery heart, trimmed and sliced

3 garlic cloves, peeled and finely chopped

1 teaspoon turmeric

1 teaspoon ground cumin

a large pinch of cayenne pepper

35 ounces canned chickpeas, drained and rinsed

2½ cups vegetable stock

1½ teaspoons sea salt

1–2 tablespoons fresh lemon juice

3 ounces green cabbage leaves

Melt 3 tablespoons butter in a large saucepan over medium heat and cook the onion and celery for about 5 minutes until softened, stirring occasionally. Stir in the garlic and spices and cook for 1 minute. Stir in 28 ounces of the canned chickpeas, add the stock and salt and bring to a boil. Simmer for 5 minutes, and then process in a blender with a tablespoon of lemon juice. If you are making it in advance, you may need to thin the soup with a little more stock before serving.

At the same time as cooking the soup, bring a medium pot of salted water to a boil, add the cabbage and simmer for 5 minutes, then drain and finely slice. Melt the remaining 2 tablespoons butter in a large pan over medium heat, add the remaining 7 ounces of chickpeas to the pan with the cabbage. Season with salt and cook for a couple of minutes. Season to taste with a squeeze of fresh lemon juice. Ladle the soup into warm bowls and serve the cabbage and chickpea mixture spooned over the top.

Ham hock and split pea soup

In France there is a thriving tradition of artisanal producers of air-dried ham. The fireplace in the kitchen of our 17th-century French farmhouse has endless nooks and hooks related to cooking. The mantlepiece is some six feet high, which is not unusual, and hams would have hung and dried in the recess.

There are still many small artisanal producers in our French neck of the woods, and one of the great joys are the cheap off-cuts of the production, namely the knuckles or uncooked ham hocks, which you can buy vacuum-packed with a "sell-by" date of several months later. They are a great fallback with a package of lentils. They need a couple of hours of cooking to render them desirably fork-tender, but what a fine job they do of releasing their gelatin and flavor into the broth. As with lamb shanks, the end result is almost entirely edible except for perhaps a thin bone.

Serves 6

1 x 1½ pound ham hock (or the equivalent of smaller ones)
4 tablespoons extra virgin olive oil, plus extra to serve
4 carrots, trimmed, peeled and thinly sliced
1 celery heart, trimmed and thinly sliced
2 medium onions, peeled and chopped
18 ounces yellow split peas
1 bay leaf
1 small dried red chile, crumbled
sea salt
coarsely chopped flat-leaf parsley, to serve

Place the ham hock in a large saucepan and cover with water. Bring to a boil, and then drain and set aside. Heat the olive oil in the same saucepan over medium-low heat, add the carrot, celery and onion, and cook for 20–25 minutes until soft and aromatic, stirring occasionally.

Rinse the split peas in a sieve under cold water, and add them to the pan. Add 2½ quarts water, the ham hock, bay leaf and chile. Bring to a boil, skimming in the process, and then simmer over low heat for 1 hour. Now cover with a lid and simmer for another hour, by which time the split peas should be nice and mushy, and the ham meltingly tender.

Transfer the ham from the pan onto a plate or chopping board, peel off the rind and shred the flesh off the bone using a fork. Add this back to the pan, and season to taste with salt – remember that the stock might be quite salty already from the ham.

Serve in warm bowls. Drizzle with oil and sprinkle with parsley. Although the soup can become quite solid once cool, it can be successfully reheated.

Peas 'n rice soup

If you keep adding stock to a risotto you eventually arrive at a soup, the difference here being that you go straight to the finishing line – which does away with the hovering over the pan. This dish is a real blaze of early summer, full of green goodies and lots of herbs.

Serves 4

4 tablespoons unsalted butter

1 bunch of scallions (about 6), trimmed and sliced into ½-inch lengths

7 ounces carnaroli rice

7 ounces shelled fresh peas

7 ounces shelled young fava beans (fresh or frozen)

½ cup white wine

6 cups chicken stock

sea salt, black pepper

2 ounces watercress, leaves and tender stems

2 ounces flat leaf parsley, leaves and tender stems

½ ounce mint leaves

3 ounces freshly grated Parmesan, plus a little extra to serve

Melt half the butter in a large saucepan over medium heat and cook the scallions for several minutes until softened. Add the rice and stir to coat it in the butter, then add the peas and fava beans and stir for about a minute. Add the wine and stock, and season with salt and pepper. Turn the heat up and bring to a boil, and then cover and cook over low heat for 15 minutes – by which time the rice should be tender.

Meanwhile, heat the remaining 2 tablespoons butter in a large pan, add the watercress and herbs and toss until they wilt. Once the soup is cooked, spoon the herbs into a food processor and add a ladle of the soup stock. Reduce to a coarse purée, and then stir this back into the soup along with the Parmesan. Adjust the seasoning before ladling into warm bowls. Sprinkle with a little extra Parmesan and serve. The soup can sit around for a few minutes, but is best eaten fairly quickly to capture the freshness of the herbs.

The Baker

Where would soup be without bread? It shares the stage — the dipping and mopping are as soothing a ritual as the soup itself. The soup you've carefully crafted deserves a co-star with the same pedigree. Putting forth some mass-produced limp slice would only drag the occasion down. A trip to the baker for an artisanal loaf is a must. In our house we can never agree whether it should be soft and white or a hearty wholegrain, which provides a great excuse for buying spontaneously. And providing the white is sturdy in character, either a sourdough or a country-style loaf, then the leftovers serve as the starting point for any number of lovely soups. It is after a couple of days have passed and the bread is a bit too dry to enjoy without toasting that it really comes into its own — part of the gratifying recycling of ingredients, that is so central to soups.

Ajo blanco

White gazpacho, traditionally eaten with grapes (although it is stunning with pomegranate seeds too), is less well known than the classic garlicky, chilled tomato variety, but it is just as traditional. Supposedly originating with the Moors, it owes its exquisite delicacy and color to almonds, which are sometimes soaked in milk before they are ground to soften them.

Ultimately it is as healthy as it is simple to make – a great pantry fallback. I always seem to have endless packages of almonds on the shelves, a result of them being a favorite ingredient in cakes. The other ingredients are no more challenging to rustle up – at most a quick trip to the corner store for a few items. All it needs is a little spot in the fridge to cool down and a little time to allow the almonds and bread to thicken the soup.

Serves 4

3½ ounces day-old coarse-textured white bread, torn up

7 ounces blanched almonds

2 garlic cloves, peeled and coarsely chopped

4 tablespoons extra virgin olive oil, plus extra to serve

1 tablespoon sherry vinegar

sea salt

½ cup white grape juice

halved red and white seedless grapes, to serve

Place the bread in a bowl and cover with cold water. Place the almonds in a food processor and process for a couple of minutes to achieve a powder consistency – by the end they should be sticking together. Squeeze out the bread and add to the food processor with the garlic, olive oil, vinegar, 2 teaspoons salt and a little cold water. Reduce to a creamy purée, scraping down the sides of the bowl as necessary. Slowly pour in the remainder of the water through the funnel with the motor running, and then add the grape juice. Transfer the soup to a bowl and adjust the seasoning – it may benefit from another half a teaspoon of salt. Cover and chill for a couple of hours, during which time it will thicken a little to the consistency of cream.

Serve the soup in bowls with a drizzle of oil. Scatter the red and white grape halves over the top and accompany with the smoked duck and an arugula salad (see below) if desired.

On the side

Smoked duck

4 ounces sliced smoked duck

Arugula salad

2 ounces arugula leaves

2 ounces roasted marcona almonds

2 ounces quince paste, sliced transparently thin

extra virgin olive oil, to drizzle

Combine the arugula leaves, roasted almonds and slivers of quince paste on a plate, and drizzle with a little olive oil.

Gazpacho

If you have ever visited Andalucía in southern Spain during the summer months you will understand why gazpacho is so central to their culture. I recall one August staying in an apartment in Seville without air-conditioning. From late morning to early evening we would sit wilting on the terrace with our hands and feet dangling in bowls of cold water, changed every half or so as they heated up. So venturing out into the relative cool of the evening air for a bowl of gazpacho soothed in a way that no other food could have done.

Take away the name and look at the ingredients, and it is basically a puréed salad, chilled. We tend to think of gazpacho as a tomato soup, but it was originally a bread soup, most likely introduced to Spain by the Moors, with the addition of olive oil, water and garlic. Tomatoes were a later addition after the discovery of the New World in the late 15th century. In fact, the Ajo blanco (see page 152) is probably much more in keeping with the original.

When tomatoes are in season during the summer months, perfectly ripe and flavorful – which sadly is the exception rather than the rule – large heirloom varieties will make for a fabulous soup. At other times of the year, cherry tomatoes promise an intense sweetness and perfume, which is why I am inclined to use them as a default here. Any number of little frills can finish off the soup – seafood goes especially well, a spoon of crabmeat or a few clams – but a final splash of good olive oil is hard to beat.

Serves 4

2½ pounds ripe cherry tomatoes
1 cucumber, ends discarded, peeled and
*   cut into pieces*
1 garlic clove, peeled and chopped
1 heaping teaspoon medium-hot chopped fresh
*   red chile*
2 heaping teaspoons finely chopped onion

½ cup extra virgin olive oil, plus extra to serve
½ tablespoon red wine or sherry vinegar
2 heaping teaspoons sugar
2 rounded teaspoons sea salt
a grinding of black pepper
3 thick slices of day-old white bread, crusts
*   removed (about 1 cup), broken into pieces*

Place all the ingredients, except for the bread, in a blender and reduce to a purée, then pass through a sieve. You will have to do this in batches. Rinse out the blender and purée the soup again, this time with the bread. Pour into a bowl, and then cover and chill for at least one hour – but don't keep for longer than necessary. Serve with some olive oil drizzled over the top of each serving.

Ribollita

Only the Italians could get away with serving something as gloriously messy as this in the name of soup – the French would be appalled. The Italians have the upper hand here – such soups are nothing without their clichéd drizzling of olive oil. It's worth ignoring the price tag and investing in a bottle that gives you particular pleasure.

Serves 6

5 tablespoons extra virgin olive oil, plus extra to serve

1 celery heart, trimmed and thinly sliced

1 large carrot, trimmed, peeled and thinly sliced

2 leeks, trimmed and sliced

4 garlic cloves, peeled and thinly sliced

14 ounces cherry tomatoes on the vine, halved

1 x 14-ounce can of chopped tomatoes

1 small dried red chile, crumbled

4 handfuls of coarsely chopped flat-leaf parsley

2½ cups vegetable stock

½ Savoy cabbage, cored, and finely sliced

1 x 14-ounce can of cranberry or borlotti beans, drained and rinsed

1 bay leaf

sea salt

½ ciabatta loaf (about 7 ounces), torn into pieces the size of a walnut

Heat 4 tablespoons olive oil in a large saucepan over medium heat and cook the celery, carrot, leeks and garlic for about 15 minutes until nicely golden, stirring frequently.

Add the fresh and canned tomatoes to the pan with the chile and half the parsley, along with another tablespoon of oil. Simmer for about 10 minutes over low heat until well-reduced. Now add the stock, cabbage, beans and bay leaf. Bring to a boil and simmer over low heat for 10–15 minutes until the cabbage is tender. Season to taste with salt. Stir in the bread and the remaining parsley, and leave to stand for a few minutes. Serve with more olive oil drizzled over the top.

Garlic soup with a poached egg

This French classic is rustic and soul-satisfying. At its heart is a lightly poached egg on toast, soaked within a garlic-rich broth, with some strings of melted Gruyère for good measure.

Serves 4

2 heads of garlic, broken into cloves and peeled

3 sprigs of fresh thyme, plus 1 heaping teaspoon thyme leaves

1 bay leaf

3 cups light chicken stock

½ cup dry vermouth

3 tablespoons extra virgin olive oil, plus extra for brushing

sea salt, black pepper

8 slices of baguette, ½-inch thick

a dash of white wine vinegar

4 large eggs

¾ cup finely grated Gruyère

Place the garlic, thyme sprigs and bay leaf in a medium saucepan with the chicken stock, vermouth, olive oil, a heaping teaspoon of sea salt and a grinding of black pepper. Bring to a boil, and then simmer over low heat for 30 minutes. Strain the soup into a clean pan, pressing the garlic through the sieve with the back of a spoon. Add the thyme leaves and adjust the seasoning.

While the soup is cooking, preheat the oven to 375°F. Lay the slices of baguette on a baking tray and bake for 5 minutes until dried out. Remove and brush with olive oil on both sides. Return them to the oven for another 10–12 minutes until lightly golden.

Bring a large pot of water to a boil and acidulate it with a dash of vinegar. Turn the heat down low until the water is barely simmering. Stir it into a whirlpool and break in the eggs one at a time. Once they rise to the surface, remove any ragged tails of white, and cook for about 4 minutes in total.

While the eggs are cooking, reheat the soup. Place two croutons in the base of four warmed deep soup bowls. Remove the eggs one at a time using a slotted spoon and place on top of the croutons. Ladle the soup over the top. Serve the cheese separately at the table.

Bacon and sage dumplings in broth

Serves 4

Dumplings

4 ounces bacon, coarsely chopped

4 ounces fresh white breadcrumbs

2 ounces shortening

about 8 sage leaves, finely chopped

3 medium egg yolks

sea salt, black pepper

Soup

3 cups chicken stock

½ cup white wine

coarsely chopped flat-leaf parsley and freshly grated Parmesan, to serve

Place the bacon in the bowl of a food processor and finely chop it. Add the breadcrumbs, shortening, sage, egg yolks and some seasoning and process until the mixture looks sticky. Keeping the motor running, add just enough water for the dough to start to cling together in lumps. Shape the dough into balls the size of a cherry and place on a plate. Cover and chill if you are not cooking them in the near future.

To cook the dumplings, bring the stock and wine to a boil with a little salt in a large saucepan and simmer over low heat for 15 minutes. Add the dumplings and poach over low heat for 10 minutes. Ladle into bowls and serve scattered with parsley, and lots of Parmesan.

Turkish village soup with bread and caraway

From Sam and Sam Clark's cookbook *Casa Moro*, which explores the cooking of Spain and the Muslim Mediterranean. Try to cook your own beans – they are a world apart from canned in this recipe.

Serves 4

8 tablespoons extra virgin olive oil, plus extra to serve

1 large onion, finely chopped

3 large carrots, trimmed, peeled and finely chopped

4 celery stalks, finely chopped

sea salt, black pepper

4 garlic cloves, peeled and thinly sliced

3 level teaspoons caraway seeds

3 tablespoons coarsely chopped flat-leaf parsley

1 x 14-ounce can of whole plum tomatoes, drained of the juice and broken up

18 ounces white cabbage, thinly sliced and chopped

5 cups water (or 4 cups water and 1 cup leftover bean liquid)

14 ounces cooked borlotti or pinto beans (7 ounces dried weight), or 2 x 14-ounce cans

½ pound day-old ciabatta or sourdough bread (crusts removed), torn into bite-sized pieces

Heat the olive oil in a large saucepan over medium heat, add the onion, carrot, celery and a pinch of salt and gently cook for 15–20 minutes until the vegetables begin to turn golden, stirring occasionally. Add the garlic, caraway seeds and half the parsley and cook for 1–2 minutes, then add the tomatoes. Cook for another 5–8 minutes, again stirring occasionally. Add the cabbage and water (or water and bean liquid) and bring to a boil. Simmer over low heat for 20 minutes until the cabbage is almost cooked. Add the beans and simmer for another 10 minutes until the cabbage is tender, stirring frequently.

Remove from heat, adjust the seasoning, then stir in the bread and the rest of the parsley. Leave to stand for 5 minutes. If it is too dry, add a little more liquid. Serve drizzled with extra virgin olive oil.

Here the soup plays second fiddle to the bacon dumplings, which are especially comforting balanced by a thin broth. With Parmesan and parsley in there too, this need be no more than a decent homemade stock.

Oven-baked French onion soup

This takes a French onion soup to its logical extreme. This is as much to do with the croutons and molten cheese as it is with any liquid. Here they are layered with a few onions with just enough stock to cover.

Serves 4

1 tablespoon unsalted butter
3 medium onions, peeled, halved and
    thinly sliced
½ cup white wine
1 quart chicken or beef stock

sea salt, black pepper
2 tablespoons brandy
5–6 slices of sourdough bread, from a small loaf,
    toasted
¾ cup grated Beaufort

Melt the butter in a large saucepan over medium heat and cook the onions for 20–30 minutes until they are a deep, even gold, stirring frequently. It's really important to take your time here and not rush them. Add the wine and simmer until well-reduced, then add the chicken stock and some seasoning. Bring to a boil and simmer over low heat for 10 minutes. Stir in the brandy. The soup can be made well in advance.

Preheat the oven to 425°F. Pour about a quarter of the hot soup over the base of a large casserole dish. Lay 2–3 slices of toast on top and pile on half the cheese. Ladle over two-thirds of the remaining soup and repeat with the rest of the ingredients. Place in the oven for 15 minutes until the cheese and toast on top are golden and sizzling. Serve immediately.

Beans on toast soup

The charm is in the comforting double whammy of carbs – here creamy white beans with thick slabs of toast, soaked in a light broth sharpened with tomatoes. A shower of Parmesan or Pecorino is always good.

Serves 6

2 tablespoons extra virgin olive oil, plus
    extra to serve
1 onion, peeled and finely chopped
2 shallots, peeled and finely chopped
1 garlic clove, peeled and finely chopped
1 celery heart, thinly sliced
1 tablespoon thyme leaves
1 x 14-ounce can of chopped tomatoes

11 ounces dried cannellini beans,
    soaked overnight
7 ounces ripe cherry tomatoes on the vine, halved
1 small dried red chile, crumbled
6 cups chicken or vegetable stock
sea salt
6 thick slices of day-old sourdough bread, toasted
freshly grated Parmesan or Pecorino, to serve

Heat the olive oil in a large saucepan over medium-low heat and cook the onion, shallot, garlic, celery and thyme for 5–10 minutes until nice and soft, without allowing the vegetables to brown. Add the canned tomatoes and simmer until well-reduced. Put in the soaked beans, cherry tomatoes, chile and stock and bring to a boil. Skim off any foam and simmer over low heat for 1¼ hours or until the beans are meltingly tender. Season with a little salt.

To serve, reheat the soup if necessary and ladle over thick slices of toast drizzled with oil. Finish with a final drizzle of oil and accompany with grated Parmesan or Pecorino.

Pappa al pomodoro

Should you find yourself in Umbria during the summer, this tomato and bread soup seems like such an obvious dish to make with the proceeds of a morning's shopping trip. You can leave the tomatoes in the sun to soften and draw out their sweetness and juices, and you'll be pleased to discover the rather hard unsalted bread that might have seemed like a challenge at breakfast holds its own in a liquid medium.

Serves 4

3½ pounds ripe beefsteak tomatoes
8 tablespoons extra virgin olive oil
3 garlic cloves, peeled and finely chopped
1 teaspoon sugar

sea salt
2 handfuls of basil leaves, torn
4 thick slices of slightly stale coarse-textured
  white bread

Bring a large pot of water to a boil, cut out a cone from the top of each tomato and plunge them into boiling water for about 20 seconds – you may need to do this in batches. Transfer them to a bowl of cold water, slip off the skins and coarsely chop the flesh.

Heat half the olive oil in a medium or large saucepan over medium heat, add the garlic and cook for a minute or two until it starts to brown. Add the tomatoes, the sugar and some salt. Give everything a stir, cover with a lid and simmer over low heat for 15–20 minutes until softened and soupy.

Add ⅓ cup water, the basil and the remaining olive oil and gently heat through. Meanwhile, toast the bread. Ladle the soup over the bread in shallow bowls, and serve with a plate of antipasti (see below) on the side, if desired.

On the side   *Antipasti*

4 slices air-dried ham
3 ounces black olives
1 x 5-ounce buffalo mozzarella, cut into wedges

Arrange the ham, olives and mozzarella in piles on a plate or board.

Bread sides

Especially crispy croutons

These crisp golden croutons are a classic for scattering over pretty much any soup.

day-old white bread, cut into slices ½-inch thick

peanut oil, for shallow frying

Cut the crusts off the bread and dice it, using a sharp chopping knife rather than a bread knife which will tear the crumb. Heat a few teaspoons of oil in a pan until it is hot enough to immerse a cube of bread in bubbles. Add a single layer of croutons to the pan and fry them, tossing occasionally until they are evenly golden and crisp. Remove them with a slotted spoon and drain on paper towels. Leave to cool. These croutons are at their best the day they are made.

Oregano croutons

These oven-baked croutons are a little lighter on the oil than the above, and flavored with dried oregano.

4 ounces day-old white bread (crusts removed), cut into ½-inch dice

3 tablespoons extra virgin olive oil

1 heaping teaspoon dried oregano

Preheat the oven to 375°F. Toss the bread in a large bowl with the olive oil and the oregano. Spread the croutons on a baking sheet and bake for 12–15 minutes until golden. Leave to cool.

Plain garlic bread

It's hard to beat garlic bread made with high-quality butter laced with sea salt crystals, good plump cloves of garlic and a well-crafted baguette.

4 tablespoons softened high-quality, salted butter

2–3 garlic cloves, peeled and crushed to a paste

small baguette

Blend the butter with the crushed garlic. Thickly slice the baguette, leaving the pieces attached at the base, and generously spread either side of each slice with garlic butter. Alternatively, slit the baguette in half lengthways and spread top and bottom. Wrap in foil and bake for 15 minutes in a 375°F oven. Open up the foil and cook for another 5 minutes to crispen the crust.

Slightly more sophisticated herby garlic bread

A little less rustic than the above, with lots of herbs to enhance the experience.

4 tablespoons softened high-quality, salted butter

6 tablespoons chopped soft herbs (e.g. parsley, chives, chervil, cilantro and/or tarragon)

1 garlic clove, peeled and crushed to a paste

small baguette

Blend the butter with the herbs and garlic. Prepare and cook as for the Plain garlic bread above.

Rarebits

Mini rarebits are great with any number of soups, but especially those in the Greengrocer chapter, and lentil ones too. Or you could make them larger and pile a mustardy green salad on top to follow the soup, which turns it into a more complete meal.

Serves 6

6 slices day-old white bread
Rarebit mixture
1½ ounces day-old white bread (crusts removed)
9 ounces sharp Cheddar, cut into chunks
2 tablespoons unsalted butter

3 tablespoons stout
1 teaspoon Dijon mustard
1 teaspoon Worcestershire sauce
1 medium egg

Place the bread for the rarebit mixture in the bowl of a food processor and blend into crumbs. Add all the remaining ingredients for the mixture and process into a paste. You can make this well in advance, in which case transfer it to a bowl, cover and chill it.

Toast the bread and cut into triangles or smaller pieces, leaving the crusts on. Spread them thickly with the rarebit mixture and place on a baking sheet. You will need to broil them under medium-low heat to cook the inside of the mixture – about 5 minutes or until the tops are nice and brown.

Pita toasts

Things on toast are always a good way of rounding out a bowl of soup. Any combination of these will make for an elegant lunch.

Slit two pita breads in half using a sharp knife, and toast them on either side under a broiler. Cut each piece into three or four strips.

Paprika, thyme and olive oil
Drizzle *a little olive oil* over the toasts, dust with *paprika* and sprinkle with *thyme leaves*.

Feta and dill
Mash *7 ounces feta cheese* in a bowl with *3 tablespoons extra virgin olive oil* and *a tablespoon of chopped dill*. Pile this mixture onto the toasts and drizzle with a little more olive oil. You can serve these cold, or toast them under the broiler until the cheese is soft and starting to turn golden.

Pea and chorizo
Simmer *7 ounces fresh or frozen peas* in boiling water for 2–3 minutes or until tender; drain. Process to a coarse purée in a blender with *4 tablespoons olive oil*, *a little salt* and *a squeeze of fresh lemon juice*. Transfer the mixture to a bowl and stir in *1–2 finely sliced scallions*, and *1 ounce sliced chorizo*, cut into thin strips. Pile this onto the toasts and drizzle with a little more olive oil.

Cocktail shortbreads

One dough, three types of cracker. These are a good way of turning a relatively plain bowl of soup into something more elaborate.

Serves 10

Dough
5½ ounces all-purpose flour
3 ounces ground almonds
10 tablespoons salted butter, chilled and diced
Flavorings
1 heaping teaspoon poppy seeds, plus extra
* for rolling*
finely grated zest of 1 lemon

1 heaping teaspoon sesame seeds, plus extra
* for rolling*
½ teaspoon ground cumin
1 ounce freshly grated Parmesan
cayenne pepper
vegetable oil, for brushing

Place the flour, ground almonds and butter in the bowl of a food processor and briefly process into fine crumbs – it's important to stand by the "briefly" here otherwise you'll end up with a dough.

Divide the mixture between three bowls. Stir a heaping teaspoon of poppy seeds and the lemon zest into one bowl, a heaping teaspoon of sesame seeds and the ground cumin into the other, and the Parmesan and a pinch of cayenne pepper into the third bowl. Bring each mixture together into a ball using your hands.

Form the cheese dough into a rough sausage shape about 1 inch in diameter, wrap in plastic wrap and give it another roll to smooth it out. Wrap the remaining two balls of dough in plastic wrap. You can freeze the doughs at this point, otherwise chill them all for an hour or two.

Preheat the oven to 300°F and brush a couple of baking sheets with oil. Knead the poppy seed dough until it is pliable, and then divide the mixture into balls slightly smaller than a cherry. Roll them in poppy seeds in a small bowl, and arrange spaced slightly apart on one of the sheets. Repeat the process with the sesame seed dough, this time rolling the balls into slightly elongated shapes and coating them in sesame seeds. Slice the roll of cheese dough into discs about ½-inch thick. Bake the biscuits for 35–40 minutes until the cheese ones are lightly golden, by which time the others will also be cooked. Loosen the cheese biscuits with a palette knife, and leave them all to cool. They will keep well for up to a week in an airtight container.

Stocks

It is a rare soup that can hold its head high with no more than water as its foundation, although there are exceptions, chilled soups such as gazpachos and others that contain enough cream or yogurt to distract from a stock's absence. Hence the majority of recipes in this book call for a broth or stock that gives the soup ingredients a platform on which to shine.

Undoubtedly the best stock will be one that is made with your own two hands. While it is tempting to turn to a packaged broth, rest assured the process couldn't be easier. I most often turn to chicken stock, I find it to be the most useful, so I always make a pot as a rule of thumb after enjoying a roast chicken with my family. I have also become a big fan of the Deluxe chicken stock (see page 171), where you not only end up with a beautifully succulent poached chicken and lightly cooked pot vegetables, but two sets of stock – the first being the cooking liquid, with a second stock being made from the carcass once you've stripped the chicken.

Of course there are those instances when buying a store-bought stock or bouillon cubes may become necessary – but contrary to what we might hope for and expect, the first is not necessarily better than the second.

What flavor?

The principal stocks called for in these recipes are either chicken or vegetable, fish stocks and very occasionally beef. Of these, I only make chicken from scratch on a regular basis, even though I have provided recipes for making vegetable and fish stocks should you choose to do so. If you do happen to find yourself in possession of a lovely pile of beef or veal bones, then simply apply the same method as for chicken. I have never had any success making lamb stock – it is difficult to successfully rid it of fat, and the end flavor tends to be disappointing. I find the same goes for duck, while pheasant results in a stock I find too strong. However guinea hen and turkey are both excellent alternatives to chicken. A stock made with ham hocks or the cooking liquid from poaching a ham both provide an excellent base for lentil and dried pea soups, providing they are not too salty.

Packaged stocks and broths

While a fresh stock is likely to be superior to bouillon cubes if it is homemade, many store-bought stocks and broths are actually inferior to cubes or powder. Sadly what began as an excellent form of convenience, has been hijacked by some of the larger food producers, whose "fresh" stocks today contain even more flavor enhancers and chemicals than the dried varieties – they have simply been reconstituted. It is the same difference as a carton of freshly squeezed orange juice and one that has been made from concentrate, especially if that juice has been packaged and sold in a way that deceives the consumer into thinking they are buying the real thing.

So when shopping for stocks and broths, always read the label to check the ingredients, and beware excessive salt and of the addition of flavor enhancers and preservatives. Bear in mind that if it is not up to snuff, you may do better with a good brand of a dried variety.

Of all the packaged stocks and broths out there, I find the organic varieties to be preferable for they use the best and most simple of ingredients. Kitchen Basics also produces a solid line of cooking stocks, providing a bit more character than many of the broths with which it shares its shelves.

Bouillon cubes and powders

The main caution with dried stocks lies in the amount and type of salt they contain. Aside from the obvious problem of unwittingly adding more salt to a soup than you intended, the type of salt contained in cubes and powders is nothing to write home about. Used in any quantity, poor salt can infuse an artificial, almost chemical, flavor into the soup. But most soups do need some salt to bring out their character, and the cleanest flavor will be provided by a good type of sea salt such as Celtic. So, when possible, go for a bouillon cube or powder that advertises "low sodium" or "no added salt," but otherwise it is best to go easy and only use them in small amounts, or alternatively make them only half of the suggested strength.

This said I wouldn't be without a pot of Marigold Swiss vegetable bouillon, that in addition to the standard comes in various forms – organic, vegan, and reduced salt, which is what I prefer. Knorr bouillon cubes are also a useful route to beef, lamb, chicken and fish broths, bearing in mind their hefty sodium content.

Basic chicken stock

Any household for whom a roast chicken or guinea hen is a regular occurence is well-situated here. By making a pot of stock a ritual at the end of the meal, the foundation for the next one is in place. And when they aren't on the menu, many butchers will be happy to give you the chicken trimmings or a carcass for the task. In this case it is worth roasting the bones first until any skin or flesh is golden, as this provides half the flavor. If, however, you find yourself paying for the trimmings, which I never feel is quite in the spirit of things, then I would rather roast and enjoy a tray of chicken wings instead.

Vegetables aren't essential but can be included if you happen to have odds and ends lying around. It makes sense to pop any half-decent trimmings into the pot, but it won't suffer unduly if you don't. What does make a difference is a drop of white wine.

1 chicken carcass, post-roast
a small glass of white wine
sea salt

Place the chicken carcass in a pot that will hold it snugly, add the wine and enough water to cover by about 1 inch. A great deal of the art lies in bringing it to a boil. It is fine to do this over high heat, but reduce it to low before it comes to a boil, otherwise you risk a cloudy (aka "greasy") stock. There is nothing more unappetizing than a pot of murky stock in the fridge, it should be a lovely crystal gold.

So having brought it almost to a simmer, skim off any foam on the surface. Add a good teaspoon of salt and simmer for at least 1 hour, longer if you prefer. Strain the stock and taste it. If it seems at all thin, then pour it back into the pot and cook at a rolling boil to reduce its volume. This will concentrate the flavor. Leave it to cool, then cover and chill. If you want to keep it longer than a few days, then simply bring it back to a boil which will kill off any bacteria likely to taint its flavor. A jellied stock is always a good sign that you have a good rich broth. Either way skim off any fat from the surface before using it.

Deluxe chicken stock

I can but look with envy at the Spanish who can buy special packages of ingredients ready for the stock pot – a selection of vegetables, chicken trimmings, a pork knuckle perhaps and cuts of veal or beef. One of the most delicious soups I have eaten lately was at the house of a Mallorcan, Maria Font, who used such a stock as the basis for "dirty rice," spiced with a local pork blood sausage *butifarron* and another chile one called *sobrasada*, with rice and shreds of chicken and pork loin that cooked in with the stock, and with all sort of vegetable goodies but in particular she includes artichokes and fava beans.

When a stock is this good, it has any number of potential lives thereafter as the starting point for adding other ingredients, either in the Mallorcan tradition or in a Japanese one with noodles and a few lightly fried or grilled ingredients, some sliced scallions or fresh herbs. Or looking to Italy with some fluffy dumplings or gnocchi and a shower of Parmesan.

In the absence of such stock-pot materials, I struggle with the idea of sacrificing a whole chicken to the pot, not unusual in professional kitchens, but here you get a delicious *poule au pot* thrown in, or, simply a great deal of very fine stock, and delicate shreds of chicken and vegetables that can be presented at the table in any number of ways.

For those with time on their side (it takes four hours in a very low oven, although just minutes to assemble), it is a fine investment. The stock itself is superb, golden and lightly jellied once chilled. Cooked at such a low temperature it does not boil or simmer in the usual fashion, which can risk the fat boiling back into the broth and muddying the flavor and appearance. I normally allow a 3½ pound chicken for four people, so figure a 4½ pound bird will serve six.

1 x 3½ - 4½ pound free-range chicken, untrussed
peanut oil for coating
sea salt, black pepper
2 good-sized carrots, trimmed, peeled and
*   thickly sliced diagonally*
1 celery heart, trimmed and thickly
*   sliced diagonally*

2 leeks, trimmed and thickly sliced diagonally
1 head of garlic, top sliced off
a few sprigs of thyme tied with string
1 bay leaf
¾ cup white wine
crème fraîche and coarsely chopped flat-leaf
*   parsley to serve for a* poule au pot

Preheat the oven to 250°F. Heat a large pan over medium-high heat, lightly coat the chicken all over with oil using your hands, season and sear to brown it on all sides – this will provide a little extra flavor for the broth.

Place it in a large heavy-bottomed pot and surround it with the vegetables and herbs, add the wine and 5½ cups water, and a little seasoning. Cover and pop into the oven for 4 hours, by which time the bird should be meltingly tender. By making it a day in advance, you can leave it to cool and then chill it, which allows for skimming off any fat on the surface before using it. Otherwise, using the lid, pour out the cooking liquid and skim off any visible fat on the surface.

If, however, you want to make a classic *poule au pot*, then use only 3 cups water, and boil to reduce by about a third to concentrate the flavor, then pour this back over the chicken and vegetables. Carve the bird and serve in warm shallow bowls with the vegetables and juices, with a large dollop of crème fraiche on top and lots of parsley scattered over the top.

Vegetable stock

A vegetable stock is the quickest of brews, and here you can add all your treasured finds to the pot with impunity. The vegetables are cooked for a mere 15 minutes, therefore you can purée them afterwards with lots of extra virgin olive oil or salty butter, and you will have a lovely sauce to serve with grilled lamb chops or roasted chicken. Two dishes that can be made in the time of one is always cause for celebration.

This is just a suggested list of veggies, and I would consider adding the stronger ones, like fennel and celery, in smaller quantities than the others.

2 pounds (prepared weight) of diced carrot,
*   leek, celery, onion, fennel, rutabaga,*
*   celery root, tomato*
2 garlic cloves, peeled and finely chopped

a small glass of white wine
a few sprigs of thyme
sea salt, black pepper

Place all the ingredients in a large pot, and add enough water to cover by about 1 inch. Bring to a boil, and simmer over low heat for 15 minutes. Strain, reserving the stock, leave this to cool, then cover and chill until required.

Vegetable purée

Discard the thyme and purée the remaining vegetables with some extra virgin olive oil or butter and salt. Pass through a sieve, cover and leave to cool if not using right away, then chill.

Fish stock

This one has a cultural weighting. If you are in France the wherewithal will not be a problem and trimmings are likely to be available at the fishmonger. But otherwise, if you call your fishmonger a couple of days in advance and ask them to save some trimmings for you, hopefully they will be happy to oblige.

2 pounds fresh fish trimmings (heads and bones),
*   sole, flounder, shellfish, etc.*
1 cup white wine
1 onion, peeled and chopped

1 clove
a squeeze of fresh lemon juice
a few parsley sprigs
sea salt

Place the fish trimmings in a large pot with the wine, add enough water to just cover and bring slowly to a boil. Skim the stock and add the onion, clove, a squeeze of lemon juice, the parsley and a little salt. Simmer the stock for 30 minutes, then strain. Leave to cool, then cover and chill until required.

Soup-making kit

Blenders

When buying a blender, check that the lid does actually screw or lock into place. This may mean going for function over looks, but it is a small price to pay. One manufacturer who seems to understand the importance of this design feature is Vitamix. But otherwise, a company's customer service department should be able to provide you with a recommendation.

www.vitamix.com

Food processors

While a good blender is the means to achieving a silky smooth soup, the food processer comes increasingly into play with the rise in appreciation of textured soups. I especially love soups that offer an array of textures, where you set aside some of the vegetables, and pulse the remainder, before combining the two. I have long been dependent on my Cuisinart. It's as close as I am ever likely to get to an assistant.

www.cuisinart.com

Immersion blenders

One of the quickest routes to puréeing a soup is a immersion or hand blender, providing you are happy with a little texture, as they never purée to the silky finish of a blender. This compact, convenient little gem saves a lot of time and cleanup.

www.amazon.com

Storage

Lock & Lock containers that have wings on the lid that clip onto the base, the original of their type, are indispensable to the soup cook. Great for storing stocks in the fridge, transporting soups and for freezing them, you can rest assured that not so much as a drop of liquid will find its way out.

www.locknlockplace.com

Index